Pirates &
Pompoms

LAURENCE KING

Published in 2016 by
Laurence King Publishing

361–373 City Road
London EC1V 1LR
United Kingdom
T +44 20 7841 6900
F +44 20 7841 6910

enquiries@laurenceking.com
www.laurenceking.com

© Text 2016 Stella Bee and Jemma Bell

Location photography: Danielle Owen
Models: Danielle Defreitas-Francis,
Amaya Edward, Sylvie Erskine,
Jaiden Warren-Halil supplied by
Daisy & Dukes Ltd; Mylie Perrina
and Dominic Winn
Flat photography: Ida Riveros
Design: Evelin Kasikov

Stella Bee and Jemma Bell have
asserted their right under the
Copyright, Designs, and Patent Act
1988, to be identified as the
Authors of this Work.

A catalogue record for this
book is available from the
British Library.

ISBN: 978-1-78067-743-9
Printed in China

Pirates & Pompoms

How to Make Children's Toys and Costumes

Stella Bee & Jemma Bell

Laurence King Publishing

Contents

Pirates

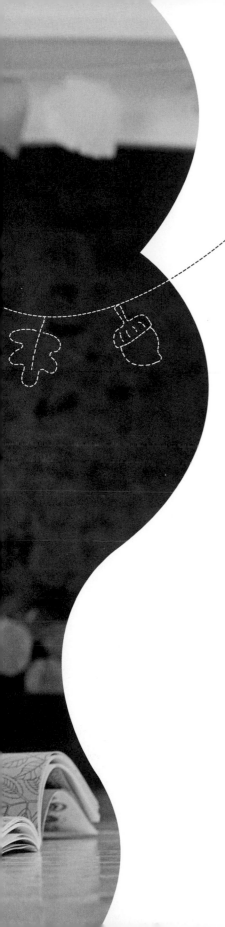

Introduction

Our own childhoods and a nostalgia for lost times inspired this book. Our parents were resourceful, creative and imaginative with their making, giving us treasured memories of playfulness, surprise and love. We want to share something of that with you, so that you too can pass this on to your little ones.

The children's toys and crafts industry is often overwhelmed by the world of mass-produced plastic and throwaway objects. And at times, children are bombarded with an overload of television and computer games. This book, on the other hand, endeavours to give you, the 'maker' – that is, parent or minder – the tools to create long-lasting, quality toys and costumes that will be used more than once; objects made with mindfulness.

All that inner pirates, ringmasters or foxes require is the time and space for their imagination to become a reality… And this book shows you how that can be achieved.

Divided into three sections – Pirates, Circus and Woodland animals – the book focuses on themes that both boys and girls can immerse themselves in. With projects covering a range of costumes, props and toys, each chapter enables a whole world to come to life for the lucky wannabe adventurers and entertainers. Our hope is that these pages will give you a helping hand in tapping into the natural and curious energy of little ones, while creating something beautiful, handmade and one-off.

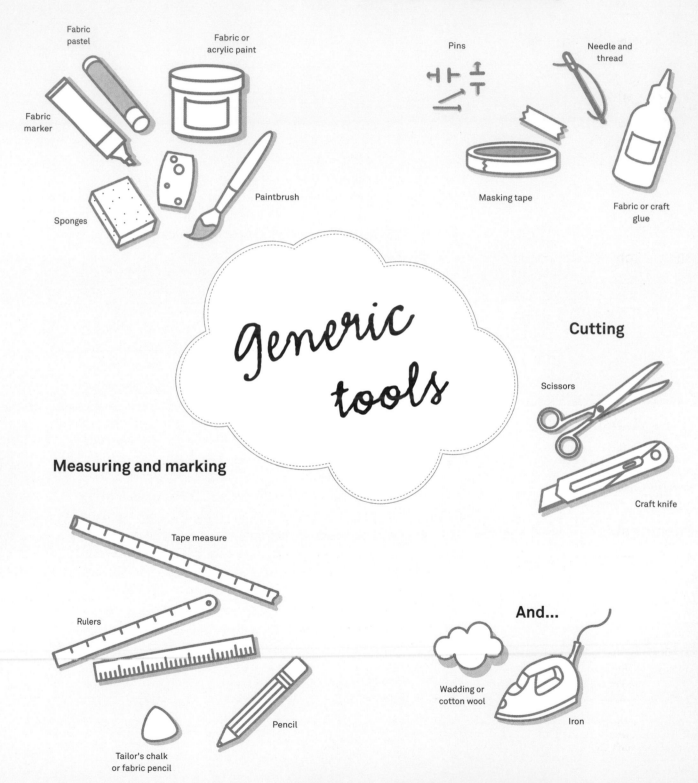

Decorating

Fabric pastel

Fabric or acrylic paint

Fabric marker

Paintbrush

Sponges

Sewing, sticking, fastening

Pins

Needle and thread

Masking tape

Fabric or craft glue

generic tools

Cutting

Scissors

Craft knife

Measuring and marking

Tape measure

Rulers

Tailor's chalk or fabric pencil

Pencil

And...

Wadding or cotton wool

Iron

Sewing

YOU WILL NEED

Needle and thread
Scissors

Working side

The side you want to be seen at the end. For example, if your fabric is printed, the working side is the side with the print.

Starting off

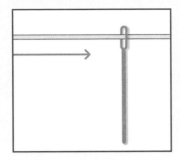

1 Thread the needle.

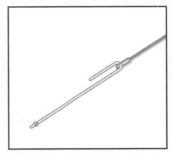

2 Knot the end of the thread. If the weave of your fabric is loose, you may want to double-knot the thread.

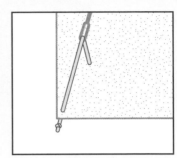

3 Start so that the knot of your thread won't show. If you have two layers of fabric, hide it between them, otherwise leave it at the back of your work.

Backstitch

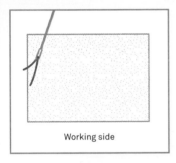

Working side

1 Start from the back or inside of your work where the knot of the thread won't show. Sew a single running stitch.

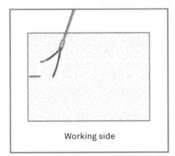

Working side

2 Bring your needle out a stitches width from the last stitch.

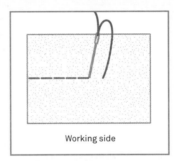

Working side

3 Place the needle through the end of the previous stitch. Repeat steps 2 & 3.

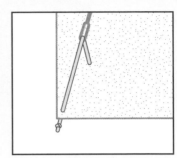

Back of your work

4 Tie off at the back or inside your work where the knot won't be visible.

Running stitch

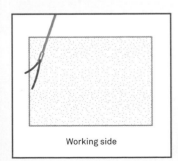

Working side

1 Start from the back or inside of your work where the knot of the thread won't show.

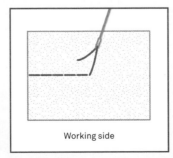

Working side

2 Try and keep your stitches an even length with an even gap inbetween.

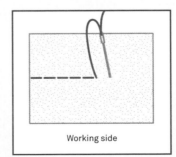

Working side

3 Tie off at the back or inside your work where the knot won't be visible.

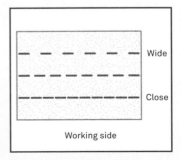

Wide

Close

Working side

4 You can use this stitch in many ways, as shown above.

Blanket stitch

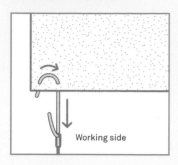

Working side

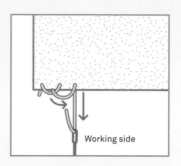

Working side

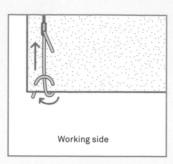

Working side

1 Sew one stitch, but don't pull it tight yet.

2 Run your needle through the loose stitch you just made and pull tight.

3 Sew another stitch the same width through the top of your fabric, but don't pull it tight.

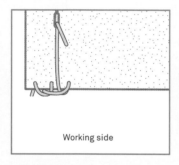

Working side

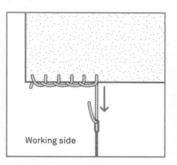

Working side

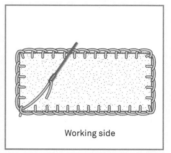

Working side

4 Run your needle through the loose stitch you just made and pull tight.

5 Repeat.

6 Thread your needle through your very first stitch, pull tight and fasten off at the back.

Hidden stitch

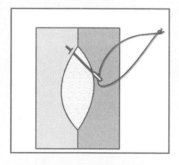

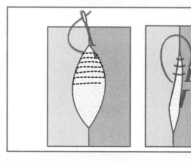

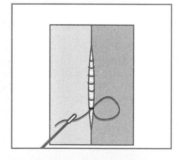

1 Thread your needle and knot the two ends together. Begin at one end of your opening, by pushing your needle and thread through one piece of fabric, up through the inside seam. Your knot should be concealed on the inside.

2 Directly opposite, on the other piece of fabric, push the needle down and back through the seam to create a small stitch. That stitch will be concealed within the seam crease. Keep repeating this step, making your way along the opening in a 'ladder'.

3 To finish, pick up a little of the last opposite stitch, pass the needle and thread under it to create a loop and then tighten to create a knot. Do this a couple of times to make it really strong. Then snip the threads and it's done.

Papier mâché paste mix

YOU WILL NEED

Craft glue
Flour
Water
Salt
Mixing bowl

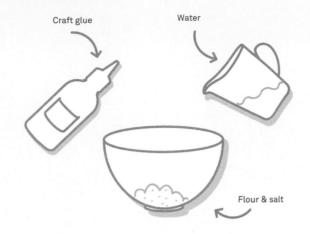

Papier mâché paste mix is made up of 1 part glue, 2 parts flour, 4 parts water and a little salt, which helps to keep the mix fresh. The mix will keep for a few days covered with cling film.

In a mixing bowl, combine ¼ cup of glue and ½ cup of flour. Slowly pour in 1 cup of water, stirring, and a heaped teaspoon of salt.

Freezer paper stencil

YOU WILL NEED

Freezer paper
Fabric paint
Masking tape
Craft knife and cutting board
Sponge
Iron

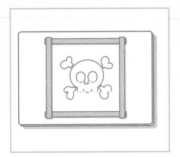

1 Print out the required template and tape to a cutting surface.

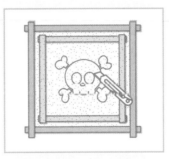

2 Cut and tape a layer of freezer paper over your template. Using a craft knife cut along the lines on the template. Keep the eyes and nose cut-outs as well as the main outline shape.

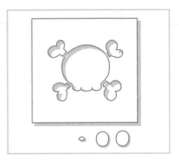

3 Remove the stencil from the cutting board.

4 Position the parts of the stencil on your fabric and iron into place. Make sure the edges are well secured by the ironing.

5 Before painting, if you are stencilling on to something with two layers of fabric, place a piece of card or a plastic bag between the two layers.

6 Apply thin layers of fabric paint with a sponge. Allow to dry between layers.

7 Carefully peel off the freezer paper. You can reuse the stencil again and again, so try not to tear it.

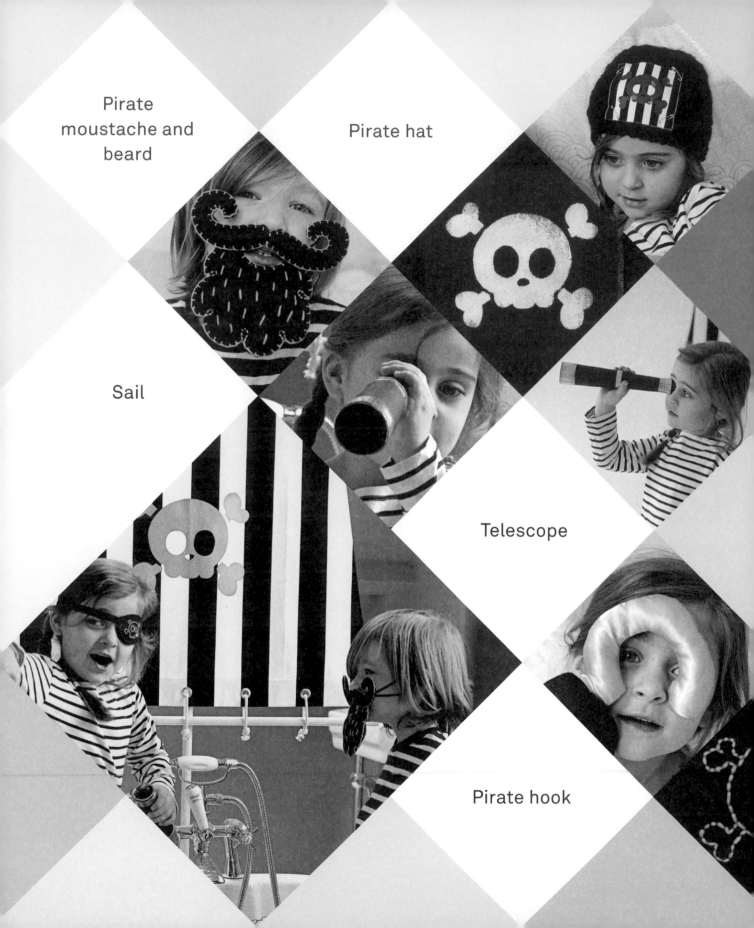

Pirate moustache and beard

Pirate hat

Sail

Telescope

Pirate hook

pirates

Wave bedhead

Mini pirate

Pirate treasure bag

Pirate eyepatch

pirate moustache and beard

YOU WILL NEED

- Prepared templates (page 134)
- Two pieces of felt or fleece (or any other fabric that won't fray at the edges, such as suede or leather): 7 x 40 cm (2¾ x 15¾ in) and 16 x 30 cm (6¼ x 12 in)
- Elastic
- Wadding or cotton wool
- Embroidery needle and about 1.85 m (6 ft) brightly coloured embroidery thread
- Needle and thread
- Scissors
- Pins
- Dressmaker's carbon paper
- Hard pencil or empty ballpoint pen

Moustache →

1

Fold the felt or fleece in half along its height. Roughly cut out the template and pin to the fabric. Carefully cut out the moustache, pinching together the two layers of fabric close to the line to get a clean cut.

2

Unpin and remove the template. Then re-pin the two sides of the fabric together. Using an embroidery needle and the coloured embroidery thread, sew the two sides together using blanket stitch, starting in the centre of the moustache.

3

As you come to the end of the first side, remove the pins and stuff a little wadding or cotton wool in between the two halves – not too much, just enough to give the moustache a little shape. Use a ballpoint pen or the wrong end of a pencil (nothing sharp) to help you push the stuffing to the end of the moustache.

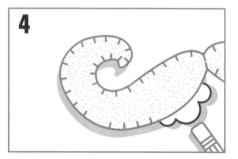

4

Continue sewing in blanket stitch. When you get close to the end of the second half, stuff this side of the moustache too.

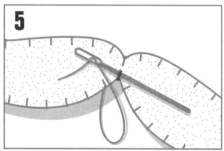

5

Thread the final stitch through the first stitch and fasten off your stitching on the back of the moustache.

Beard →

1

Lay a piece of carbon paper over one end of the fabric and lay the template on top. Pin around the edges of the design, and trace over the beard pattern with a hard pencil or an empty ballpoint pen.

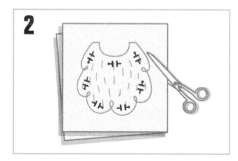

2

Remove the template and carbon paper, fold the fabric in half and pin the two layers together around the inside edge of the beard shape. Cut around the lines, pinching together the part you are cutting with your fingers.

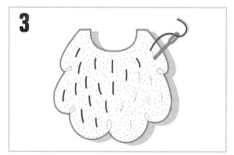

3

If you would like to add the extra texture details, unpin the two sides and stitch the details on one side of the beard. This will become the front of the beard.

4

Sew the elastic in position on the back piece of the beard using the matching cotton thread.

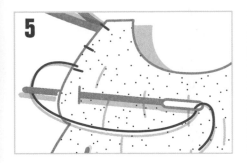

5

Line up the two sides of the beard and pin together. Using the embroidery thread, blanket-stitch the two sides together starting at the outer left-hand corner.

6

At each valley crease, stop using blanket stitch and use running stitch to create a loop. Then continue with blanket stitch until the next join. When you have stitched almost all the way around, stuff the beard (see Moustache step 3 opposite), then complete the stitching.

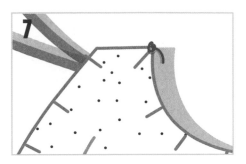

7

Fasten off. This won't be seen, as it will be under the moustache, so don't worry about hiding it.

Join together →

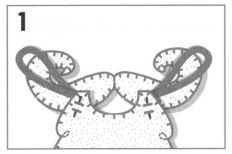

1

Pin the moustache and beard in your chosen position.

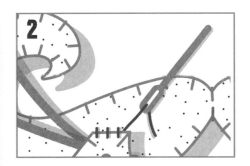

2

Stitch them together using the matching cotton thread. Fasten off.

pirate eyepatch

YOU WILL NEED

- Prepared templates (page 134)
- 10 x 20 cm (4 x 8 in) piece of black felt
- Black elastic
- Embroidery needle and brightly coloured embroidery thread
- Needle and thread
- Scissors
- Pins
- Tape measure
- Dressmaker's carbon paper
- Hard pencil or empty ballpoint pen

TIP

Duplicate the Pirate eyepatch template found on page 134, as you might want to use it again.

1

Pin the patch template to a double layer of black felt.

2

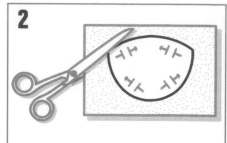

Cut out the shape, being careful to keep the two layers of felt together.

3

Place one of the eyepatch pieces on a hard surface. Place a little square of carbon paper and the eyepatch skull and crossbones design in the centre. Trace the image using a hard pencil or an empty ballpoint pen.

4

Using brightly coloured thread, embroider the skull design using backstitch.

TIP

Little stitches will make the design more accurate, especially on the curves.

5

Measure the elastic to fit your little pirate's head. Make sure it grips securely but is not too tight.

6

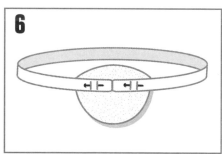

Pin the elastic to the inside of the back piece of the eyepatch, making sure it isn't twisted.

7

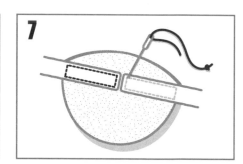

Stitch the elastic in place using black thread. Start and finish stitching on the inside, so your knot doesn't stick out at the back.

8

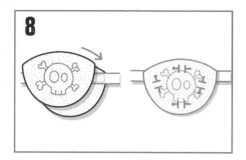

Pin the two layers of felt together.

9

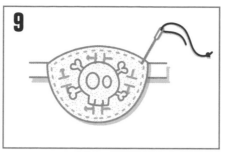

Using black thread and running stitch, sew them together about 3 mm (⅛ in) in from the edge.

10

When you've finished stitching, fasten off between the layers.

11

Now put the eyepatch on your pirate and let them run around yelling 'Aha, me hearties!'

Shiver me timbers!

pirate hat

YOU WILL NEED

- Prepared template (page 134)
- 9 x 9 cm (3½ x 3½ in) piece of fabric
- Woolly hat
- White or gold fabric paint
- Small gold safety pins
- Freezer paper
- Craft knife and cutting board
- Masking tape
- Iron

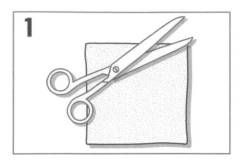

Cut out your 9 x 9 cm (3½ x 3½ in) piece of fabric. The edges don't need to be perfectly straight.

Using the template, make a stencil from freezer paper (see page 11).

Roughly centre the stencil on the felt, and iron it in place.

Apply fabric paint in thin layers using a sponge.

Peel off the stencil when dry.

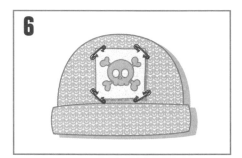

Using the safety pins, attach the felt to the hat.

TIP

You can use leather, suede or waxed cotton – or any other fabric that doesn't fray at the edges – in place of the felt.

pirate hook

YOU WILL NEED

- Prepared templates (page 134)
- 4 pieces of black felt, each 10.5 x 16 cm (4 x 6¼ in)
- 34 x 25 cm (13½ x 10 in) piece of silver fabric
- Approx. 30 cm (12 in) length of 15 mm (½ in) ribbon
- Wadding or cotton wool
- Needle and silver or grey thread
- Black thread
- Scissors
- Pins
- Tailor's chalk or fabric pencil
- Ruler

Hook →

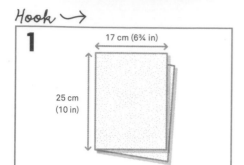

1

17 cm (6¾ in)

25 cm (10 in)

Fold the silver fabric in half.

2

Lay the hook template on the fabric and draw around it using tailor's chalk or fabric pencil.

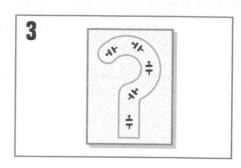

3

Pin the two layers of fabric together.

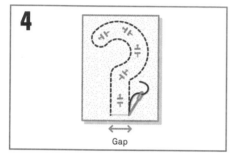

4

Gap

Sew along the traced line in backstitch using silver or grey thread, leaving the bottom open.

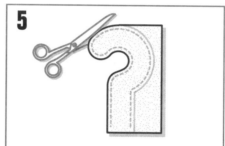

5

Cut the excess fabric off, leaving 1–1.5 cm (½ in) around the stitching.

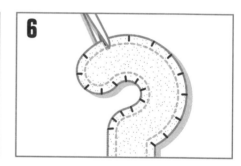

6

Snip little cuts into the curved edges. Do NOT go right up to the stitching; leave a gap of a few millimetres.

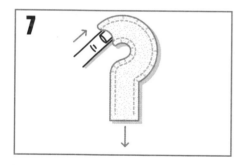

7

Turn inside out. Poke your finger in the very end of the hook and push through to the open end.

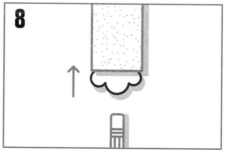

8

Stuff tightly, using a pencil to help get the stuffing to the end.

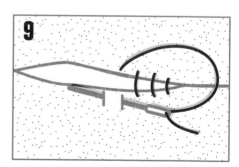

9

Sew the bottom seam using hidden stitching.

Hook cuff →

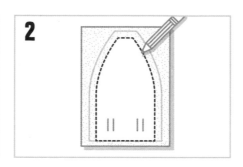

1 10.5 cm (4 ⅛ in)
16 cm (6¼ in)

Lay the hook cuff template on the felt and draw around the solid line using chalk or fabric pencil. Repeat for the other three pieces of felt.

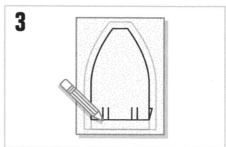

2

Cut along the dotted line of the template, reposition on the felt and draw around. Repeat for all four pieces.

3

Fold the template to the bottom of the cut indicators, and mark with a dot on all four pieces with tailor's chalk or fabric pencil.

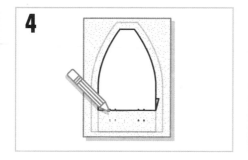

4

Fold the template to the top of the cut indicators, and mark with a dot on all four pieces with tailor's chalk or pencil. Using a ruler, join the dots. Repeat for all four pieces.

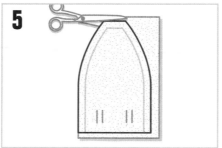

5

Cut off the excess fabric from all four pieces.

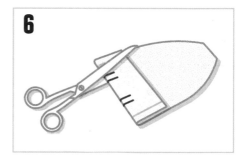

6

Fold halfway up the marks and snip. Repeat for all four pieces.

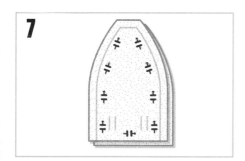

7

Pin two of the cuff pieces together, marked sides out.

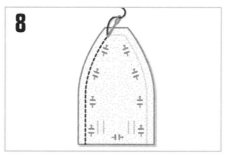

8

Sew together along the dotted line on just one side, using backstitch and black thread.

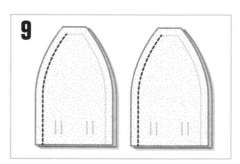

9

Repeat steps 8 and 9 for the remaining two cuff pieces.

10

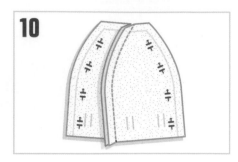

Line up the edges of the two sewn cuff parts and pin together.

11

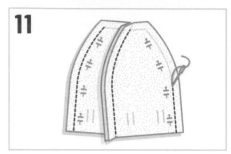

Use backstitch to sew the two sides together, leaving the top and bottom open.

Join together →

1

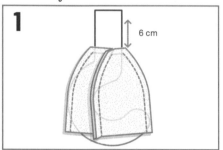

6 cm

Position the hook in the hole at the top of the cuff, leaving 6 cm (2 ½ in) sticking out. The cuff should still be inside out.

2

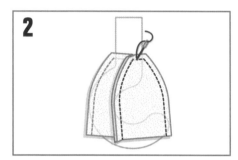

Using backstitch, sew the cuff to the hook, sewing along the top line.

3

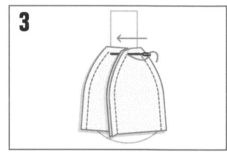

Thread the needle through when you get to each seam. Make the stitches strong and tight.

4

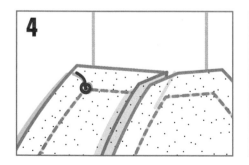

Fasten off.

5

Turn the right way out and thread ribbon through the cuts.

6

Tie the hook on to your little pirate's hand and do pirate things!

Blow me down!

Sail

YOU WILL NEED

- Prepared template (page 135)
- 92 x 82 cm (3 x 2½ ft) piece of strong fabric
- 4.75 m (15½ ft) length of 12 mm (⅜ in) rope
- 30 cm (12 in) of ribbon or other rope
- 73 cm (28¾ in) length of 25 mm (⅞ in) wooden dowel
- 84 cm (33 in) length of 25 mm (⅞ in) wooden dowel
- 14 eyelets (15 mm/½ in size)
- Iron-on webbing
- Scissors
- Freezer paper
- Tailor's chalk or fabric pencil
- Fabric paint
- Sponge
- Hammer
- 4 small nails
- Iron

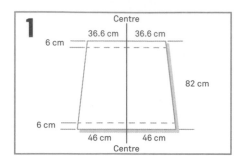

Cut to shape shown. On the reverse of the fabric, mark out two 6 cm (2¼ in) hems on the shorter sides using tailor's chalk or fabric pencil.

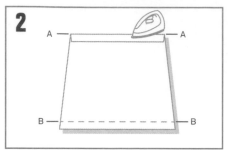

Fold along A and B, as shown, and iron in place.

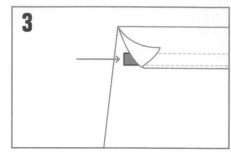

Secure the hems using iron-on webbing.

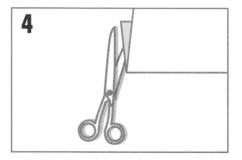

Trim off the excess webbing.

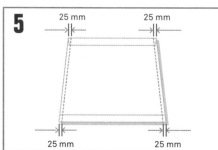

On the reverse of the fabric, mark out two 25 mm (⅞ in) hems on the longer sides.

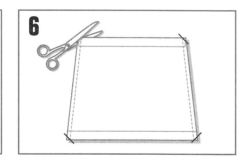

Trim the four corners of the fabric, as shown.

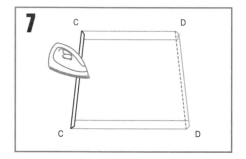

Fold along C and D, and iron in place.

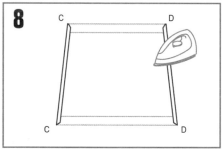

Secure the hems using iron-on webbing.

For the skull and crossbones, prepare a freezer paper stencil (see page 11) using the template.

10

Iron the stencil in place in the centre of the sail. Dab on fabric paint sparingly with a sponge. Allow to dry, and add another coat of paint if you need to.

11

Once dry, carefully peel off the stencil.

12

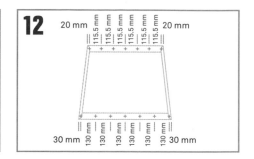

On the reverse of the flag, measure and mark as shown. Follow the instructions on the pack to attach the eyelets at each mark.

13

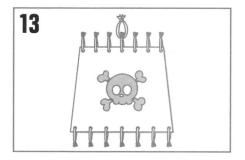

Thread the rope through each eyelet and knot. Thread the ribbon through the middle rope loop and knot. This can be used to hang the sail from a hook or nail.

14

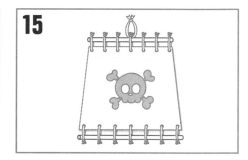

Measure and cut wooden dowel, sand the ends if needed.

15

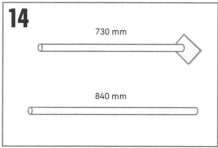

Thread the wood through the rope loops.

16

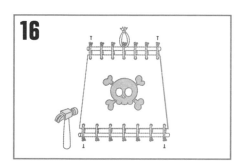

To stop the flag sliding off, use small nails to attach the end loops to each dowel.

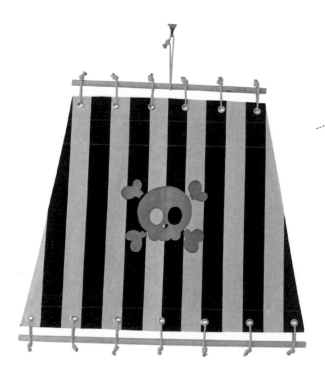

Weigh anchor and take to the high seas!

Telescope

YOU WILL NEED

- Prepared templates (page 135)
- 2 cereal packets, ideally made from grey card
- Cardboard tube
  (such as the inside of a roll of tinfoil)
- Newspaper and papier mâché paste mix (page 11)
- Scissors
- Glue stick
- Fine sandpaper
- Masking tape
- Plastic bag
- Black and gold paint
- Paintbrush

Main telescope parts →

1

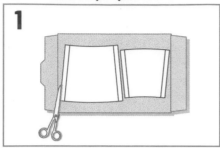

Glue the large cone and small cone templates to the plain side of a large section of cereal packet, and cut them out.

2

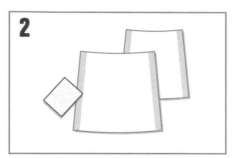

Sand the edges of both templates on the glossy side; this is where they will be glued together.

3

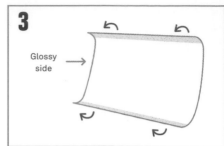

Glossy side →

Ease the sides of both templates so that they curve.

4

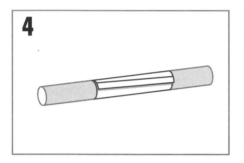

Keeping the glossy side in, roll each template around the cardboard tube.

5

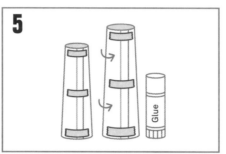

Glue

Align the lines and tape both templates into position.

Cone holders →

1

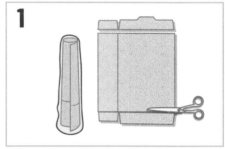

Cut the flaps off half a cereal packet. Roll into a tight tube and place in the plastic bag.

2

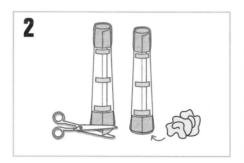

Push this tube inside the larger taped cone, and allow it to spring outwards to fit the cone. Fill with scrunched-up newspaper and cut the base so it stands up. Repeat steps 1 and 2 for the smaller cone.

3

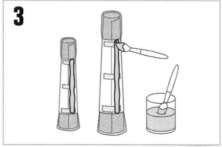

Make some papier mâché paste mix (see page 11) and add some to the joins of the two cones.

4

Tear strips of newspaper 2–3 cm (1 in) wide. Add two layers of newspaper strips to the cones using the paste mixture, keeping it even and smooth. Allow to dry.

Telescope detail →

1

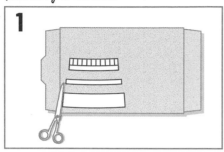

Glue and cut out the eye piece and two cone templates from the cereal packet, as before.

2

Sand the glossy sides so that they will glue more easily.

3

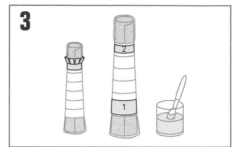

Glue the new parts in place. Apply two layers of papier mâché paste and allow to dry.

4

Trim the ends with scissors. If needed, paste the large cone ends, and allow to dry.

Eye piece →

1

Insert the small cone into the large cone and extend. Apply two layers of papier mâché paste to the eye piece, allow to dry, and repeat. Leave until fully dry.

Paint →

1

Lightly rub down both cones with fine sandpaper. Paint the central sections black and the details gold.

Ahoy there, me hearties!

mini pirate

YOU WILL NEED

- Prepared templates (page 136)
- 32 x 16 cm (12½ x 6¼ in) piece of plain, heavy fabric, such as canvas
- 32 x 16 cm (12½ x 6¼ in) piece of patterned, heavy fabric, such as striped canvas
- 3 pieces of black felt: approx. 10 x 10 cm (4 x 4 in), 4 x 3 cm (1½ x 1⅛ in) and 8 x 20 cm (3 x 8 in)
- 30 cm (12 in) length of ribbon, no wider than 3 cm (1⅛ in)
- 2 buttons (use one or two bright colours!)
- Wadding or cotton wool
- Embroidery needle and black embroidery thread, or fine black fabric pen
- Embroidery thread in a colour to match your chosen ribbon
- Needle and black and white thread
- Scissors
- Pins
- Tailor's chalk or fabric pencil
- Fabric glue
- Dressmaker's carbon paper
- Hard pencil or empty ballpoint pen

Pirate body →

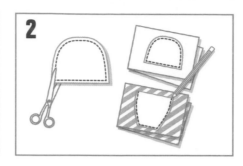

1

Fold each piece of canvas in half, working side facing inwards. Lay the pirate's head template on the plain fabric and his body template on the striped fabric. Draw around the solid line of the templates using tailor's chalk or fabric pencil. Pin both sides of the fabric together just outside the traced solid line.

2

Cut along the dotted lines of the printed template. (Note that there is no dotted line at the top of the trousers.) Align the newly cut templates within the previously traced shapes on the fabric and draw around them. The inner line is the guide to follow when sewing the two sides together, and the outer line is the cutting guide.

3

Cut the folded fabrics following the outer solid line. Pinch the two layers of fabric together as you cut. When you've finished cutting, remove the pins. You now have four pieces of fabric: two to form the head and two to form the body.

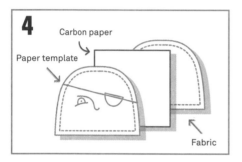

4

Carbon paper

Paper template

Fabric

Sandwich the carbon paper between the head template and one piece of the 'head' fabric, place on a hard surface and line up the three layers. Trace the face using an empty ballpoint pen or hard pencil, pressing hard.

5

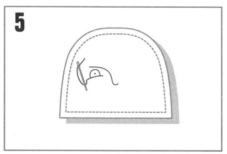

Using running stitch, embroider the face details using black embroidery thread. Alternatively, use the fine black fabric pen to draw on these details.

6

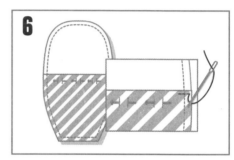

Join the head and body, working sides up, and pin into place with the patterned fabric overlapping the 'head' fabric by about 1 cm (½ in) and backstitch together. (This stitching will not be visible on the finished toy.) Repeat this step with the other two pieces of fabric.

7

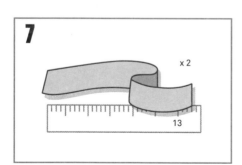

x 2

13

Cut two pieces of ribbon, each 13.5 cm (5¼ in) long, for the pirate's sash. Melt the ends using a match or your stove to stop them fraying.

8

Pin the ribbon in place and stitch to the sides of the body using running stitch. Make sure the side stitching on the ribbon is outside the seam line, as shown.

Moustache and beard →

1

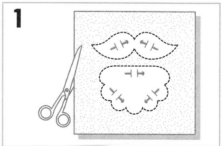

Pin the moustache and beard templates to the 10 x 10 cm (4 x 4 in) piece of black felt, and cut out the shapes.

2

Pin the beard in place and stitch on using running stitch along the top edge.

3

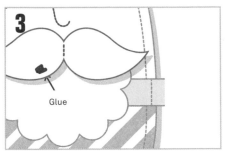

Glue

Attach the moustache using fabric glue. You can also add a couple of stitches down the middle to make it really secure.

Eyepatch →

1

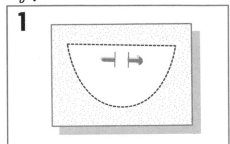

Pin the eyepatch template to the smallest piece of black felt (4 x 3 cm/1½ x 1⅛ in), and cut out the shape.

2

Pin the eyepatch in place and sew all the way around the patch using running stitch. Then, using running stitch, embroider the band of the eyepatch at an angle along the top of the patch. Alternatively, use the fine black fabric pen to draw the band.

Tattooed arms →

1

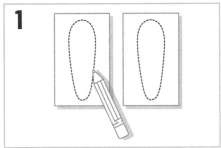

Lay the two prepared arm templates on two separate pieces of plain canvas fabric and draw around them using tailor's chalk or fabric pencil. Cut out the arm pieces.

2

Carbon paper

Paper templates

Fabric

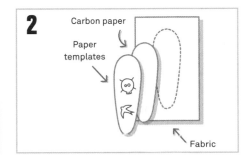

Place some carbon paper between an arm piece and its paper template. On a hard surface, trace the tattoos using an empty ballpoint pen or hard pencil to transfer the tattoo design through the carbon paper on to the fabric. Repeat for the other arm.

3

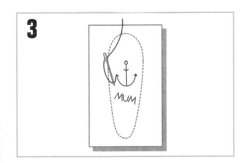

Embroider the tattoos using running stitch and black embroidery thread. Alternatively, draw over the faint lines with the fine black fabric pen.

4

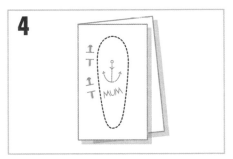

Lay the decorated arms on a piece of plain canvas fabric with the tattoos face down. Pin the fabric together. Repeat for the second arm.

5

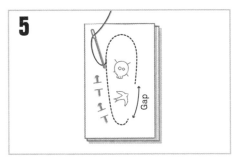

Gap

Stitch the fabric pieces together along the traced dotted line of the arm. Make sure to leave a gap, about 4 cm (1½ in) long, on one side of the arm, so that you can pull the fabric through. Repeat for the second arm.

6

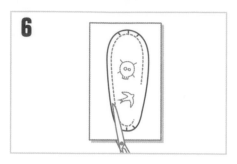

Unpin the fabric and cut around the stitched shape, about 0.5 cm (¼ in) from the stitching. Be careful not to cut too close. Then snip little cuts into the curved edges. Again, do NOT go right up to the stitching; leave a few millimetres (about ¼ in). Repeat for the second arm.

7

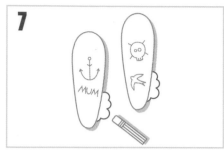

Pull the fabric through to the correct side using something blunt (such as the eraser end of a pencil) to help the ends through, and stuff each arm with wadding or cotton wool (not too much; they don't need to be stiff).

8

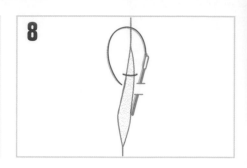

Sew up the gaps of the arms using hidden stitch.

9

Sew a button in place on each of the upper arms using the black thread. Make sure each button is nice and secure.

Complete the pirate's body →

1

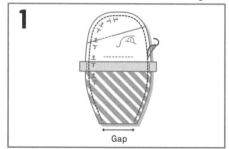

Pin the two sides of the pirate together with the right sides facing inwards, and sew the sides together along the traced dotted line. Use a tight running stitch and leave a gap of 4–5 cm (1½–2 in) at the bottom. Unpin the fabric.

2

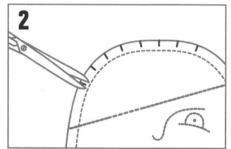

Snip little cuts into the curved edges. Do NOT go right up to the stitching; leave a few millimetres (about ¼ in).

3

Pull the fabric through the gap you left when sewing the sides together. Now attach the arms to the pirate by sewing through the buttons and securing on the inner side of the body fabric. We've attached our arms at the ribbon 'waistline'.

4

Once the arms are attached, stuff the body with wadding or cotton wool. Then sew up the gap by carefully folding in the edges and using hidden stitch. Fasten off the stitching between the two sides.

5

To give the pirate some 'legs', backstitch a 5 cm (2 in) line from the bottom of his body, running up the centre, using black thread. Go through both sides of the pirate and his stuffing.

pirate hat →

1

Fold in half the 8 x 20 cm (3 x 8 in) piece of black felt. Pin on the pirate hat template and cut around it, being careful to keep the two layers of felt together so that the two cut pieces are identical.

2

Carbon paper   Fabric

Paper templates

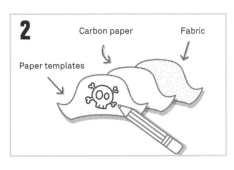

Unpin the template and sandwich carbon paper between one side of the hat and the hat template. Trace the skull and crossbones.

3

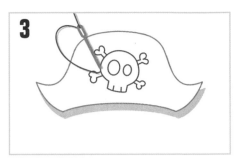

Embroider the skull and crossbones in coloured thread, using backstitch.

4

Re-pin the two sides together with the right sides facing outwards. Using running stitch, sew the two sides together with the black cotton thread. Use small stitches for a clean finish. Fasten off between the two layers to keep it neat.

5

Pin the hat on to the pirate and sew it on in a few places to prevent it from falling off. Use black thread and keep your stitches small. Fasten off between the two pieces of hat fabric.

pirate treasure bag

YOU WILL NEED

- Prepared template (page 135)
- 30 x 35 cm (12 x 13¾ in) piece of cotton fabric
- String or thin rope
- Needle and thread
- Scissors
- Pins
- Freezer paper
- Iron

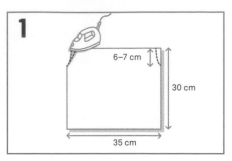

1

On the two shorter sides of the piece of cotton, fold and iron down a 'hem' from the corners, approximately 6–7 cm (2½ in) long and 1 cm (½ in) wide.

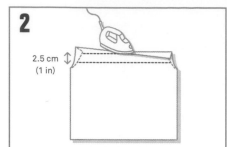

2

Measure 1 cm (½ in) from the top of the fabric and then fold and iron flat. Measure 2.5 cm (1 in) from the folded edge and then also fold and iron flat to create a 'loop' for the drawstring.

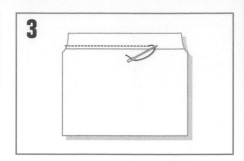

3

Starting in the middle of the fabric, neatly stitch along the bottom ironed edge, approximately 0.5 cm (¼ in) above it, using running stitch in a contrasting thread. When you reach the ends, stitch a few times to make the edges really secure. This hem is to create the channel for the drawstring.

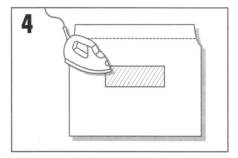
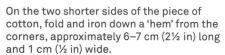

4

Transfer the label template to iron-on transfer paper, centre the design on the working (front) side of the fabric and iron it on.

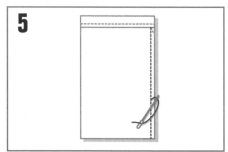

5

Fold the fabric in half with the working side on the inside, and pin. Using running stitch, stitch along the side, about 1 cm (½ in) from the edge. Do not stitch past the stitched drawstring hem, and make sure the drawstring hem meets up on both sides.

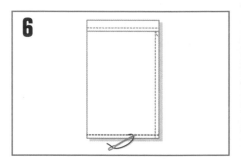

6

Stitch along the bottom edge, about 1 cm (½ in) from the edge, using running stitch.

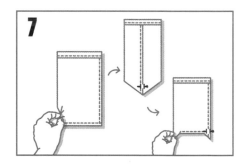

7

Pinch a corner of the stitched bag and pin together. The drawings show this step from different angles, to show how it should look. Pin about 3 cm (1⅛ in) from the bottom. Repeat for the other corner.

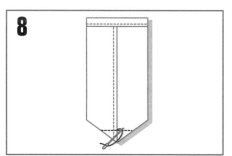

8

On the pinched corner, mark a straight horizontal line just about your pins. Sew along this line using running stitch. Repeat for the other corner. Stitch tightly and securely, especially where the stitching meets the vertical seam.

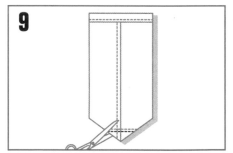

9

Cut the corner fabric just below the stitched line, about 0.5 cm (¼ in) from your stitches. This gives the bag a square base.

10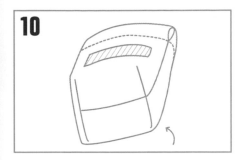

Turn the bag the right side out. The bottom of the bag should look like this.

11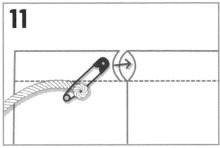

Finally, thread the string or rope through the stitched drawstring hem.

TIP

Attach a safety pin to one end of the string and slowly inch it through.

Pieces of eight!

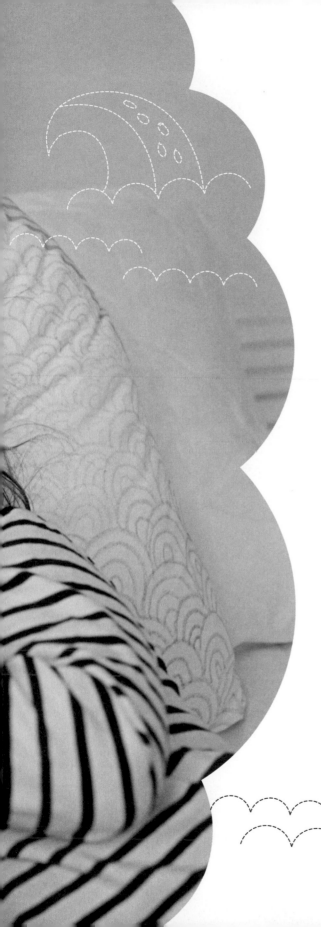

Wave bedhead

YOU WILL NEED

- Prepared template (page 136)
- 95 x 60 cm (about 3 x 2 ft) piece of plain, medium-weight fabric, such as canvas
- 95 x 60 cm (about 3 x 2 ft) piece of patterned fabric, in a similar weight to the plain fabric
- Wadding or cotton wool
- Needle and thread, or a sewing machine
- Scissors
- Pins
- Blue or green fabric marker or pastel
- Tailor's chalk or fabric pencil
- Long ruler
- Sticky tape
- Iron and a sheet of paper

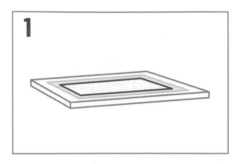

1

Lay out the plain fabric on a flat surface.

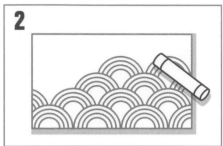

2

Draw the wave pattern on to the fabric with the marker or pastel.

● **TIP**

You can mark the pattern on first using a fabric pencil. This will wash out once you've finished. Choose a similar colour to your fabric marker or pastel, and draw lightly as a guide.

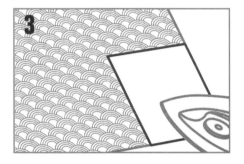

3

Once you have completed your wave pattern, follow the fabric marker/pastel instructions if necessary to make it colourfast. Cover with a sheet of paper and iron.

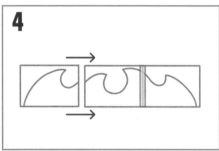

4

Join the pieces together using sticky tape.

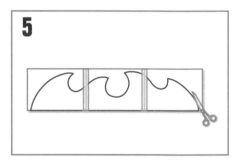

5

Cut out the template.

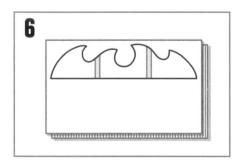

6

Lay the two types of fabric on top of each other, with the working sides facing inwards. Place the template on top, leaving a little excess fabric along each edge.

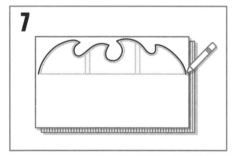

7

Using a long ruler, draw a line along the bottom and 60 cm (23½ in) up each side, always keeping at least 2 cm (1 in) in from the edge of the fabric.

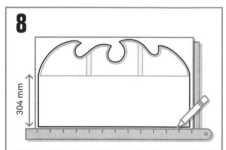

8

Draw around the top of the template using tailor's chalk or fabric pencil.

9

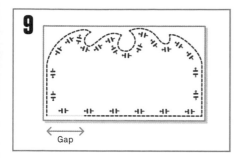

Gap

Pin the two pieces of fabric together just inside the drawn lines and sew together using tight running stitch (or machine stitch), leaving a gap of approximately 10 cm (4 in) at one of the bottom corners through which to turn the fabric right side out.

10

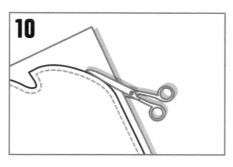

Cut the excess fabric away, leaving approximately 2 cm (1 in) outside the stitched line.

11

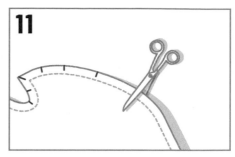

Snip little cuts into the sharp curves, no closer than 4 mm (¼ in) to the stitching.

12

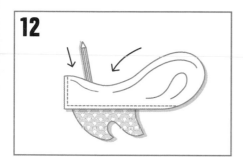

Pull the fabric through the gap to turn it right side out.

13

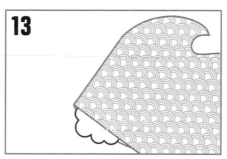

Stuff with wadding or cotton wool.

14

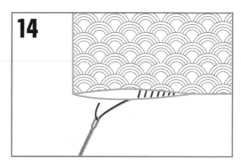

Sew up the gap using hidden stitch.

Big top

Ringmaster's coat

Strongman weights

Plinth

Ringmaster's hat

Circus

Pompom bunting

Juggling beanbags

Circus letter

Toy lion

Big top

YOU WILL NEED

- Prepared bunting template (page 138)
- 2 pieces of matt fabric 193 x 97 cm (6 ft 4 in x 3 ft 2 in)
- Hula hoop (the largest you can find)
- 4 pieces of contrasting-coloured felt, A4 size
- 1.2 m (4 ft) length of 15 mm (½ in) ribbon (for the door ties)
- 1.5 m (5 ft) length of 30 mm (1 in) ribbon (for the back ties)
- 1.94 m (6 ft 4 in) length of 15 mm (½ in) ribbon (for the bunting)
- Needle and thread, or a sewing machine
- 5 m (16½ ft) strong thread
- 12 m (39½ ft) hemming tape
- 1.84 m (6 ft) length of 38 mm (1½ in) ribbon
- Scissors
- Pins
- Permanent marker
- Tailor's chalk or fabric pencil
- Tape measure
- Saw
- Iron

Fabric →

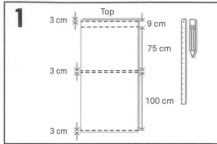

1

On the back of one piece of your fabric mark and measure as above using a tailor's chalk or pencil. Repeat this on the other piece.

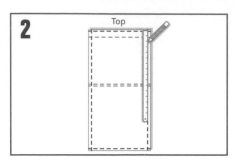

2

Measure and mark a line 2.5 cm (1 in) from each side.

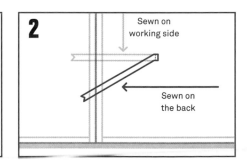

3

Fold part of the fabric over and use the original marks to mark on the working side using a soft pencil, tailor's chalk or fabric pencil. Piece 1 right side, piece 2 left side.

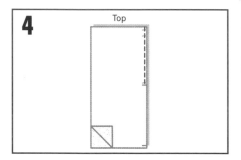

4

With the working sides facing inwards, lay the fabric pieces on top of each other. Backstitch or machine stitch 2.5 cm (1 in) from the edge, starting from the top and stopping at the fourth mark down, ie 90 cm (3 ft) from the top.

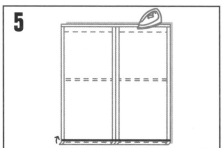

5

Open the fabric out flat (working side face down) and iron along the side marks of each piece of fabric, then secure the hems using hemming tape. Next iron and tape the top and bottom hems in the same way.

To hold the hula hoop →

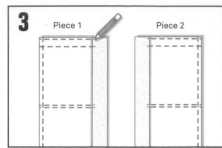

1

Turn over 3 cm (1⅛ in) at both ends of the length of 38 mm ribbon. Secure using hemming tape.

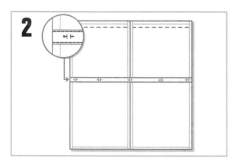

2

Line up the 38 mm ribbon with the central lines on the fabric, pin in place, and backstitch or machine stitch. Leave one end open, as shown.

Door ties and back ties →

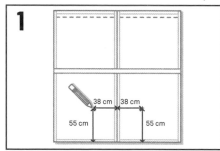

1

Measure and mark on the tent fabric, as shown.

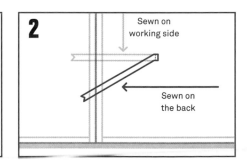

2

Use a small, tight running stitch to sew a 30 cm (12 in) piece of ribbon over your line on both sides of the fabric.

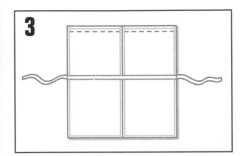

3

In the same way, sew a 1 m (3 ft) piece of ribbon to each side of the tent to form the back ties. Do not close up the hole left for the hula hoop.

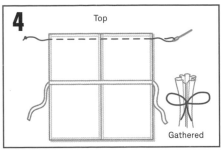

4

Top

Gathered

Using 30 mm (1 in) running stitches, sew along the remaining mark. Pull the thread tight to gather, and tie the ends in a big bow.

Bunting →

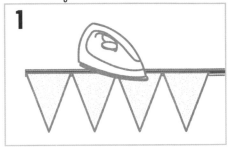

1

Using the bunting template, cut out 11 flag shapes from the felt. Position, pin (if needed) and hemming-tape the flags to the ribbon. Then, using the bottom stitching of the 38 mm ribbon across the tent fabric as your guide, pin and then stitch the bunting in place.

Hoop →

1

Pull the hula hoop apart at the join. Thread the hula hoop into the channel in the fabric until it comes out the other end. Pull the fabric tight and mark where the hoop sticks out. Remove the hoop and saw off any excess. Thread it back into the tent..

2

Tie the back ties up so the tent forms a half circle. Hang the tent up on a picture hook or picture rail.

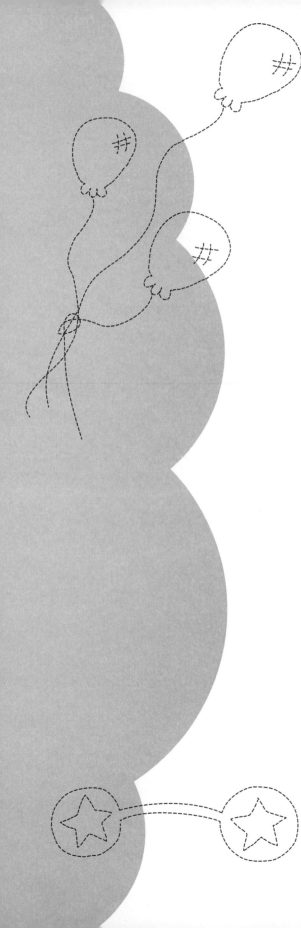

Circus letter

YOU WILL NEED

- Prepared template (page 137)
- 40 x 40 cm (15¾ x 15¾ in) piece of wood with a nice grain
- Freezer paper
- Craft knife and cutting board
- Masking tape
- Pencil
- Ruler
- Sandpaper
- Sanding block
- Acrylic paint in 3 colours
- Sponge
- Iron

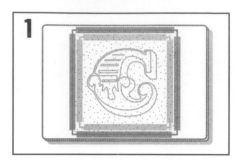

1 Place the template underneath a piece of freezer paper on your cutting board and tape down.

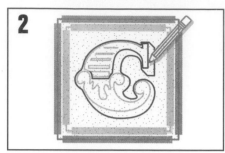

2 Trace the lines of the template in pencil on to the freezer paper.

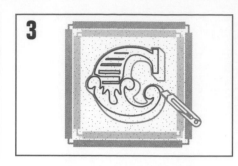

3 Cut the rectangles out using a craft knife and set aside, then cut around the inside line, as shown.

4 Cut around the outside of the letter, as shown.

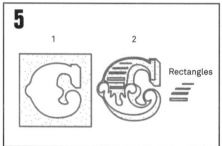

5 You now have two layers and some cut-out rectangles.

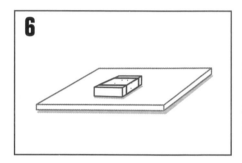

6 Sand down the wood on the front and all the edges.

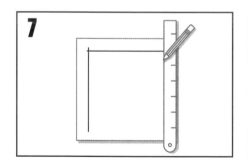

7 Draw a very light pencil line all around, a ruler's width from the edge.

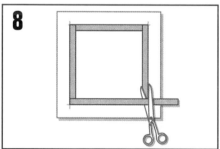

8 Place masking tape along the inside of the lines.

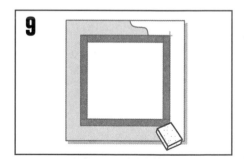

9 Using a sponge, paint around the edge – this doesn't have to be perfect. We used white.

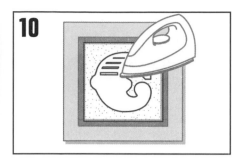

10

When dry, position layer 1 and the rectangles on to the wood, and iron in place.

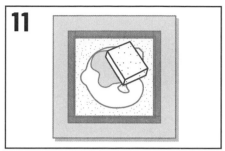

11

Using a sponge, paint over the stencils. We used white.

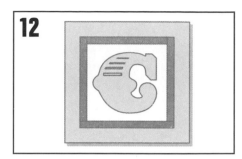

12

When dry, gently peel off the outer stencil, leaving the rectangle stencils in place.

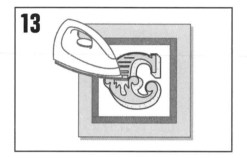

13

Position and iron layer 2.

●

TIP
You can protect your iron from the paint with a sheet of scrap paper.

14

Using a sponge, paint over the stencils. We used pink on the bottom half and teal on the top.

15

When dry, gently peel off the stencil and the masking tape.

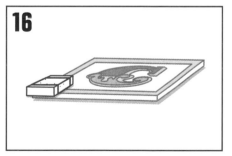

16

Lightly sand the letter and edging to give a vintage, textured look.

17

Your circus letter is finished.

TIP
Protect your letter by using matt spray lacquer. You could also light it up with fairy lights: drill holes around the edges and insert your lights.

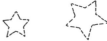

plinth

YOU WILL NEED

- Prepared star template (page 138)
- Metal bucket
- Acrylic paint in 6 colours and gold
- Paintbrush
- Scissors
- Freezer paper
- Ruler
- Pencil
- Eraser
- Masking tape
- Saw
- Hammer
- Iron or spray mount

1 Saw through the handle of the bucket, and remove it.

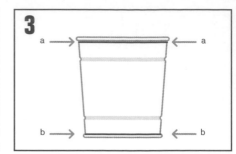

2 Use a hammer to flatten the handle tabs inwards.

3 Measure the widest point of the bucket (a). Repeat for the narrowest point (b). Divide both measurements by 10 to give you measurements A and B (a ÷ 10 = A; b ÷ 10 = B).

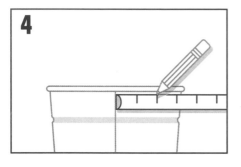

4 Just below the lip, starting at the seam, measure and mark every A cm using a pencil.

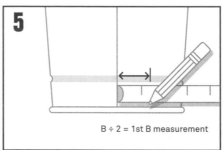

B ÷ 2 = 1st B measurement

5 For the bottom of the bucket, starting at the seam, the first measurement needs to be half of B.

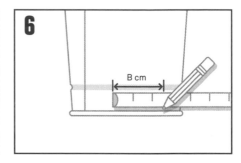

B cm

6 From here, measure and mark every B cm at the bottom of the bucket.

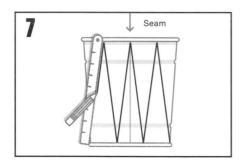

Seam

7 Join the marks to form triangles, as shown.

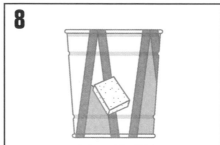

8 Stick masking tape over every other triangle. Paint the masked triangles using a sponge. Allow to dry and repeat. Once dry, carefully remove the masking tape and erase any remaining pencil marks.

TIP

Stick the masking tape at the top, get the general angle by using the bottom pencil mark as a guide, and slowly press the tape into the contours of the bucket to create a clean line.

9

Make a star stencil on freezer paper using the template. (Keep the cut-out star-shaped section, as you will need it later.) Iron or spray-mount the stencil into position, between two triangles about half way up the bucket. Paint white using a sponge.

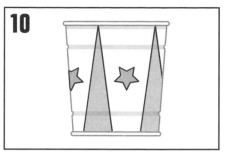

10

Allow to dry, and add a second coat of white paint if needed. Carefully peel off the stencil. Repeat until you have a star between all of the triangles.

11

Iron the star you cut out for your stencil on to the bottom of the bucket, and paint the whole of the underside.

12

When dry, peel off the star.

Roll up, roll up!

pompom bunting

YOU WILL NEED

- Prepared template (page 138)
- Thin card (such as a cereal box)
- 2 or 3 rolls of tulle ribbon 15 cm (6 in) wide, in various colours
- Narrow ribbon and matching thread
- Scissors
- Pencil
- Glue stick
- Tape measure

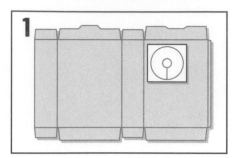

1

Glue the template to the card.

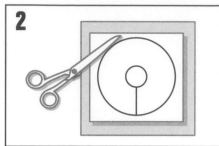

2

Cut out the circle, including the hole in the centre.

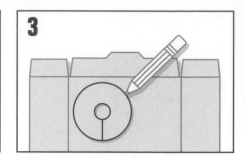

3

Draw around the circle on to the card, and cut out, so that you have two identical circles, each with a cut from outer edge to inner edge.

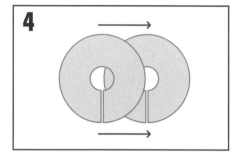

4

Line up the two circles, one on top of the other.

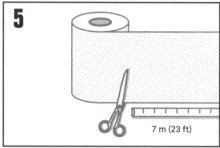

5

7 m (23 ft)

Cut a 7 m (23 ft) length of tulle.

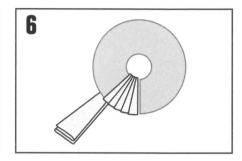

6

Starting at one side of the cut, wrap tulle around the circle. Don't worry if the tulle bunches up.

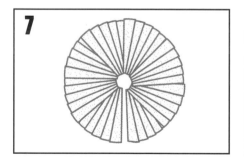

7

Cover all around, keeping it as even as you can.

8

Slot the blades of your scissors between the two layers of card and cut through the tulle all the way round.

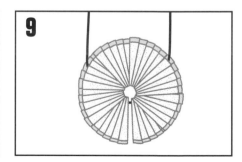

9

Cut a 30 cm (12 in) length of thread, slide it between the two layers of card and tie tightly. Wrap it around again and tie once more.

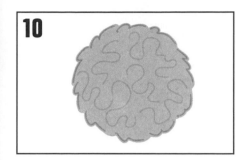

10

Remove the card.

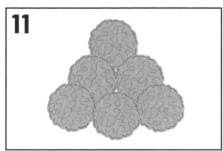

11

Whatever length of bunting you decide to make, you will need to make a pompom for every 20 cm (8 in).

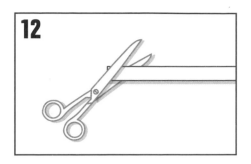

12

Cut the ribbon at a 45-degree angle and melt the ends using a match or your stove to stop them from fraying.

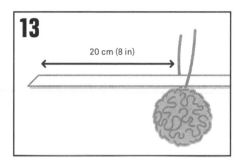

13

20 cm (8 in)

Tie the pompoms on to the ribbon roughly every 20 cm (8 in), using the matching thread.

● **TIP**
Make a two-coloured pompom by using tulle of one colour on one half of the circle and swapping to another colour for the other half.

The circus is in town!

Juggling beanbags

YOU WILL NEED

- 3 pieces of cotton fabric, each 15 x 8.5 cm (6 x 3¼ in)
- Needle and thread
- Tailor's chalk or fabric pencil
- Ruler
- Masking tape
- Fabric paint
- Sponge
- Rice

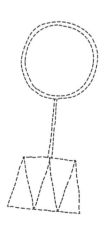

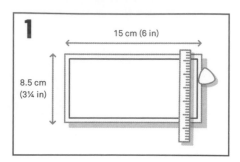

1

15 cm (6 in)

8.5 cm (3¼ in)

Measure a 0.5 cm (¼ in) hem on all four sides of one of the fabric pieces, and mark using tailor's chalk or fabric pencil. Do this on the front and back of the fabric.

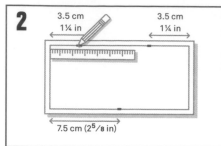

2

3.5 cm 1¼ in   3.5 cm 1¼ in

7.5 cm (2⅝ in)

With the working side facing down, mark all the measurements shown above. These measurements will form the guides for the painted triangles.

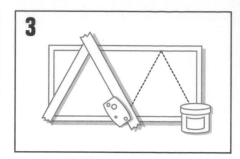

3

Mask off one triangle with masking tape, as shown, and apply the fabric paint with a sponge.

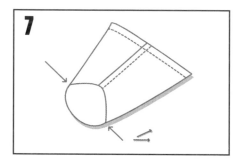

4

Once dry, peel the masking tape off, mask off the second triangle and paint in the same way.

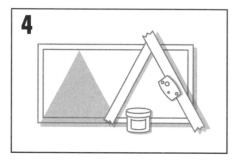

5

Fold the fabric in half, with the painted side facing in, and backstitch along the edge opposite the fold.

6

Reposition the stitched edge, so it's in the centre of the square and backstitch along the bottom, going through the two layers of fabric.

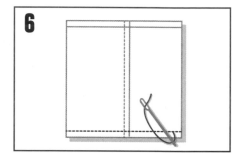

7

Push the sides together to make a pyramid, and pin.

8

Gap

Backstitch along the pinned edge, but leave a 3 cm (1⅛ in) gap at the end.

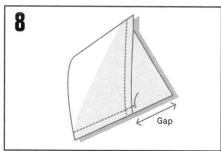

9

Paper cone

Turn the pyramid right side out and fill with rice, using a paper cone to help funnel it in.

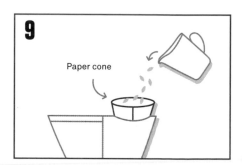

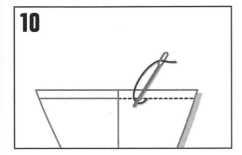

10

Use a small, neat running stitch to sew the bag closed. Repeat all steps twice more to make the second and third beanbags.

TIP

Make the Pirate treasure bag on page 47 to keep the Juggling beanbags safe. Use a fabric that matches your beanbags.

The greatest show on earth!

Ringmaster's hat

YOU WILL NEED

- Approx. 1 x 1.5 m (3 x 5 ft) piece of black velvet
- Ribbon and coloured cotton fabric, as required for decoration
- Approx. 1.5 m (5 ft) strong cardboard (from a cardboard box)
- Scissors
- Craft knife and cutting board
- Strong tape, such as duct tape
- Pencil
- Fabric glue

TIP

The hat measurements are based on the diameter of an average child's head, which is 45 cm (about 18 in).

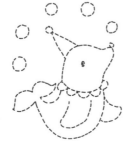

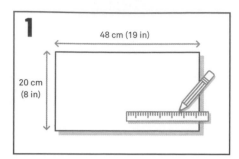

1

48 cm (19 in)

20 cm
(8 in)

Mark a rectangle 48 x 20 cm (19 x 8 in)
on the cardboard, and cut it out. This will
become the 'cylinder' of the hat.

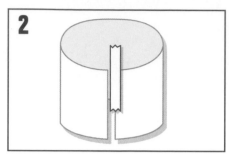

2

Roll the cardboard up and tape the edges
together securely with strong tape.

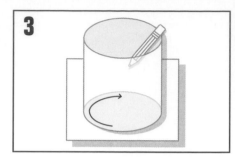

3

Sit the cylinder on another piece of
cardboard and mark the inner diameter
of the cylinder on to the bottom piece of
card using a pencil. Remove the cylinder
and cut out the marked circle.

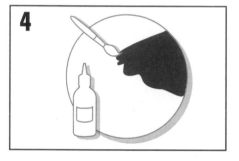

4

Apply a thin layer of fabric glue to one side
of the cardboard circle.

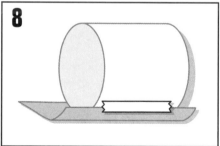

5

Stick the circle to the back of a flat, smooth
piece of velvet and allow to dry.

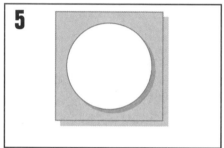

6

Trim the velvet all the way round, 2 cm
(1 in) from the edge of the cardboard.

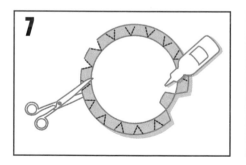

7

Snip little triangles from the edge of
the velvet and glue the tabs on to the
cardboard. Allow to dry.

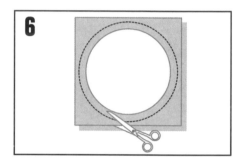

8

Lay the cardboard cylinder, on its side,
on a rectangular piece of velvet (about
54 x 26 cm/21 x 10 in). Tape one of the
short ends of the velvet to the cylinder.

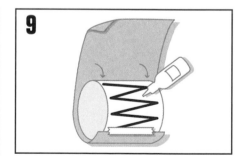

9

Cover the cardboard cylinder with glue and
roll it over so the velvet sticks to it. Where
the two ends of the velvet meet, glue them
down as neatly as you can.

10

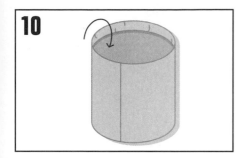

Tuck the excess velvet over the ends of the cylinder and glue it down on the inside.

11

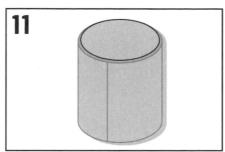

Now position the velvet-covered circle on one end of the cylinder. It should just snuggle within the walls. Apply a little glue and securely tape it in place from the inside.

12

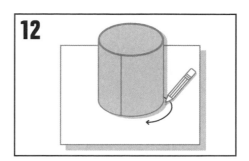

Place the cylinder on a large piece of cardboard and draw around the circle, as before.

13

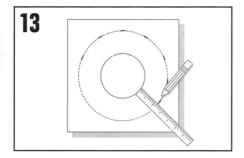

Measure and mark 7 cm (2¾ in) outside the circle at several points. Join the marks carefully to create a bigger, outer circle.

14

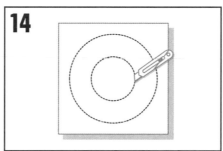

Cut out the inner circle and then the outer so that you are left with an 'O' shape.

15

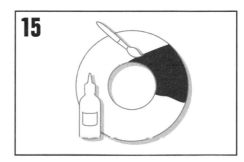

Apply a thin layer of fabric glue to the surface of the cardboard.

16

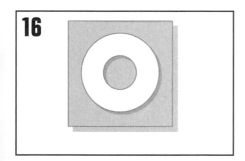

Stick the circle to the back of a flat, smooth piece of velvet and allow to dry.

17

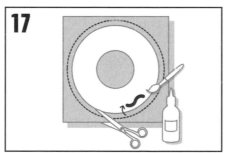

Trim the velvet all the way round, 1 cm (½ in) from the edge of the cardboard. Fold the velvet edge over the cardboard and glue down well.

18

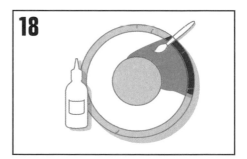

Apply a layer of glue to the back of the velvet-covered cardboard ring. Try to be neat around the velvet edges. This is the bottom of the hat brim.

19

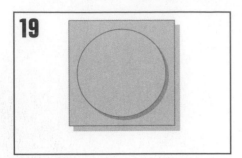

Stick the cardboard, glue side down, to a flat, smooth piece of velvet and allow to dry. Both sides of the brim will now be covered in velvet, including the inner cut-out circle.

20

Cut the velvet as close to the cardboard circle as possible, and as neatly as you can. This is the top of the hat brim.

21

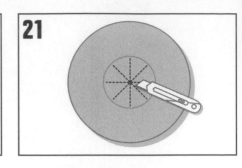

Using a craft knife and ruler, cut a series of lines through the two velvet layers in the centre, where there is no cardboard.

22

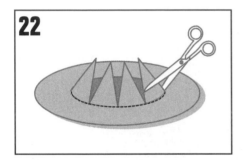

On the top of the hat brim, snip the triangles off as close to the inner circle as you can, and as neatly as possible.

23

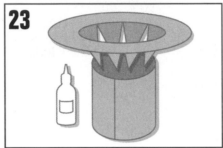

With the cylinder sitting top down, place the brim on the cylinder, with the bottom side of the brim facing up. Tuck the remaining triangles into the cylinder and glue them to the inner wall. Secure with tape on the inside of the cylinder.

24

Finally, glue on any details you want. We've added a yellow ribbon, a turquoise diamond and a red 'V' shape at the top of the hat.

Ringmaster's coat

YOU WILL NEED

- Prepared templates (pages 140–141). The templates should fit most kids' T-shirts from 3 years upwards. If your T-shirt is very tiny or quite large, you may need to adjust accordingly
- Plain T-shirt
- 3 pieces of lightweight fabric in a colour that matches the T-shirt: 50 x 50 cm (19¾ x 19¾ in), 15 x 15 cm (6 x 6 in), 6 x 10 cm (2½ x 4 in)
- 50 x 50 cm (19¾ x 19¾ in) piece of lightweight patterned fabric
- 6 or 8 buttons (depending on the size of the T-shirt)
- Needle and thread to match the T-shirt
- Scissors
- Pins
- Freezer paper
- Tailor's chalk or fabric pencil
- Craft knife and cutting board
- Masking tape
- Piece of scrap card or newspaper
- Ruler
- Black and white fabric paint
- Sponge
- Iron

Adjusting the T-shirt →

1

Iron the T-shirt.

Note: If the T-shirt is already the right length (4 cm/1½ in below their waist), miss out steps 2–4.

2

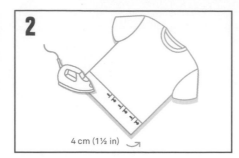

4 cm (1½ in)

Put the T-shirt on your little ringmaster and mark with tailor's chalk or fabric pencil about 4 cm (1½ in) below their waist. Take the T-shirt off your little one, then turn the bottom hem up inside, folding at the point you have marked. Iron and pin.

3

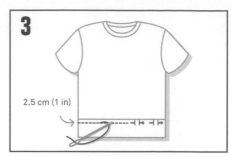

2.5 cm (1 in)

Stitch along the pinned line with stretch stitch if you have a sewing machine or loose backstitch if sewing by hand, roughly 2.5 cm (1 in) from the edge. You may want to rule a guide line with tailor's chalk. Remember to fasten on and off on the inside of the T-shirt.

4

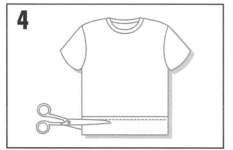

Cut off the excess fabric. The nature of the fabric means that the T-shirt won't fray.

Preparing the stencils →

1

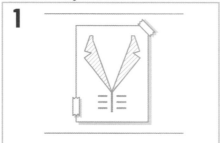

On a cutting surface, tape down the printed lapels template using masking tape. This makes it easier to cut out the stencil.

2

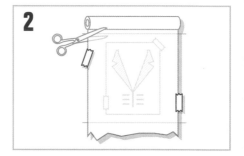

Roll out some freezer paper to fit over the template and cut to size. Stick it, shiny side down, to the template.

3

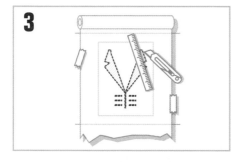

Using a ruler and craft knife, cut the freezer paper along the lines on the template. Repeat steps 1 to 3 for the white 'V' stencil template.

4

Fold the T-shirt in half along its length, place your hand along the fold and draw a line down the T-shirt using tailor's chalk. This is to help you position the stencil.

5

Lay the T-shirt flat on an ironing board and line up the freezer paper 'V' stencil. You can use a small piece of masking tape to secure it. Then iron over the freezer paper, making sure you pay particular attention to the edges. Before you paint, place a piece of card or newspaper between the two layers of your T-shirt to ensure the paint doesn't seep through to the back.

6

Using the sponge, carefully apply the paint through the stencil.

Ringmaster's tails →

1

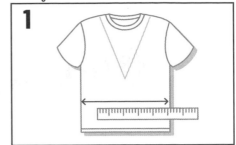

While your T-shirt is drying, you can begin to make the tails for the ringmaster's coat. Start by measuring the width of the T-shirt. Check that the tail templates fit the width of the T-shirt, and adjust if necessary.

2

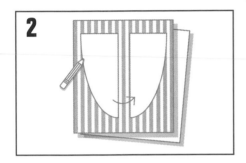

Place the patterned fabric working side down and draw around the tail template on to the fabric. Flip over the template and draw around it again. Repeat this step on the fabric that matches the T-shirt.

3

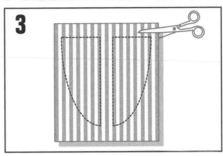

Cut out the tails, leaving a 2 cm (1 in) excess around the edge of your drawn line. You will have four tails: two patterned and two plain.

4

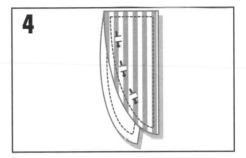

Line up and pin the piece of patterned fabric to its corresponding piece of plain fabric, with the working sides facing in. Repeat for the other two pieces of cut fabric. You will now have two 'inside-out' pinned tails. If you are using satin or slightly different fabric weights, it may be worth tacking the two sides together before sewing.

5

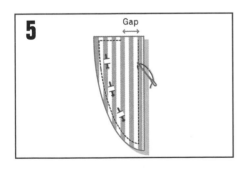

Backstitch along the drawn line using cotton thread in the same colour as your T-shirt. Don't forget to leave the gap indicated on the template for pulling the tails right side out.

6

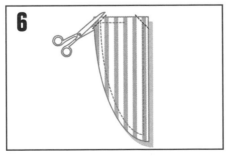

Trim the corners using sharp scissors, but don't get too close to your stitching. Turn the tails the right way out and iron along the seams.

7

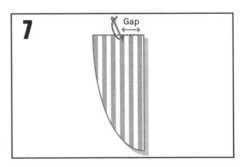

Using a sewing machine or running stitch, stitch along the gap you left. This will be on the inside of the finished coat, so it doesn't need to be too tidy.

Lapels →

1

When the T-shirt is dry, gently peel off the freezer paper. If you're careful not to tear it, you can keep it to reuse. Before starting the lapels stencil, mask the white 'V' area by running masking tape along the edges, over the white paint. This will preserve the clean edges while you are stencilling the lapels.

2

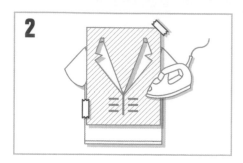

Position the lapels freezer-paper stencil on the T-shirt and iron it down. Pay special attention to the edges and sharp corners.

3

Using the sponge, carefully apply the paint to the T-shirt through the stencil. (See Tips box for ways to get a clean finish.) Leave to dry, then remove the stencil.

Note: If the bottom buttonholes are too close to the end of your T-shirt or don't fit on, don't paint them in. This will depend on the size of your T-shirt.

Bow tie →

1

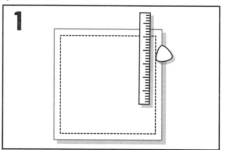

Take the 15 x 15 cm (6 x 6 in) square of fabric that matches the T-shirt. Place it working side down and draw a line 1 cm (½ in) from the edge with tailor's chalk and a ruler.

2

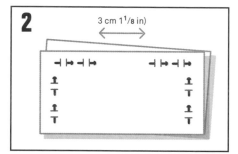

3 cm 1⅛ in

Fold fabric in half and pin. Stitch the folded fabric using running stitch, leaving a 3 cm (1⅛ in) gap in the middle of the long edge.

3

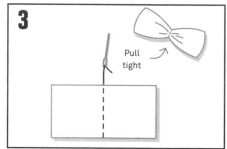

Pull tight

Turn fabric the right way out using the gap you have left. Then sew a large running stitch along the middle and pull tight to gather the centre. Fasten off. This won't be seen, so don't worry about how neat it is.

4

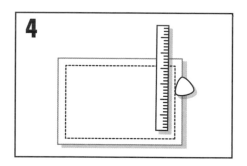

Take the 6 x 10 cm (2½ x 4 in) piece of fabric that matches the T-shirt. With the working side facing down, draw a line 1 cm (½ in) from the edge with tailor's chalk and a ruler.

5

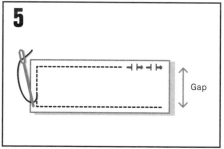

Gap

Fold fabric in half lengthways, pin together and sew with running stitch, leaving one end open. Turn the right way out by pulling the fabric through the open end.

6

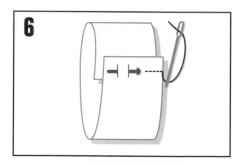

Loop fabric over and pin one end to the other. Stitch together using running stitch and matching thread.

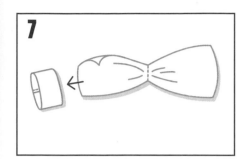

7

Feed the other part of the bow tie through the stitched loop. Once in position, carefully add a few stitches to secure the two parts.

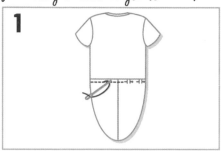

1

Pin the tails to the back of the T-shirt, using your stitched seams as a guide to keep them straight. Using backstitch, sew the tails to the T-shirt seam line. If you are using a machine, you may want to straight-stitch below the stretch-stitch seam. Remember to start and finish on the inside of the T-shirt.

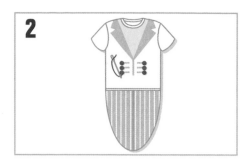

2

Sew the buttons on to the T-shirt.

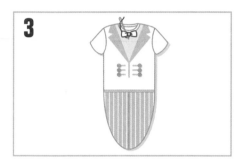

3

Stitch the bow tie in place on the T-shirt.

Come one, come all!

Strongman weights

YOU WILL NEED

- Approx. 120 cm (4 ft) long and 3-4 cm (1 ½ in) thick pole or rod
- Newspaper and papier mâché paste mix (page 11)
- Scissors
- Craft knife
- Masking tape
- Cling film
- Black and white paint
- Paintbrushes

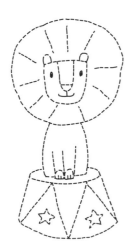

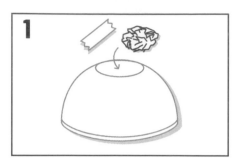

1

Take a round bowl about 20 cm (8 in) in diameter (nothing too nice) and turn it upside down. If the bowl has a flat base, scrunch up a ball of newspaper and tape it down to round it off.

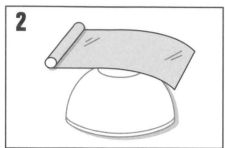

2

Cover the bowl tightly with two layers of cling film.

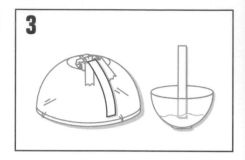

3

Make a large bowl of papier mâché paste mix (see page 11). Tear the newspaper intro strips, dip them in the mix and begin to cover the bowl. When dipping the strips slide them between two fingers to get any excess mix off the newspaper.

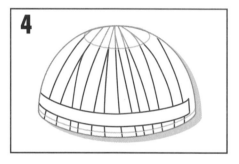

4

Build up four or five layers of newspaper strips, allowing each layer to dry completely before starting on the next. Use a combination of horizontal and vertical strips to make it stronger.

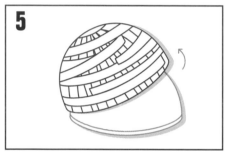

5

Once the newspaper is completely dry, prise the papier mâché off the mixing bowl. If the cling film is stuck to the papier mâché, just peel it off.

6

Repeat steps 3–5 another three times to make a total of four papier mâché hemispheres. Neaten the edges by cutting off any stray bits of paper with scissors.

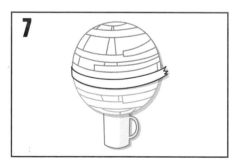

7

Tape two hemispheres together securely with masking tape, sitting the bottom hemisphere on a cup to help hold it still. Repeat with the other two hemispheres. You'll now have two complete spheres.

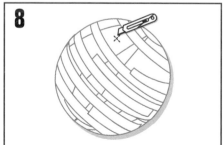

8

Using a craft knife, cut a cross into the surface of each papier mâché sphere, roughly the diameter of the pole, and lift the triangle points outwards. Avoid doing this on the taped areas.

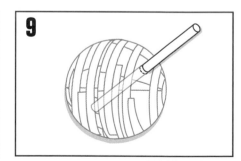

9

Insert the pole through the cut cross, all the way into the sphere, so that it touches the opposite side, and tape it into place with masking tape. Attach the second sphere to the other end of the pole.

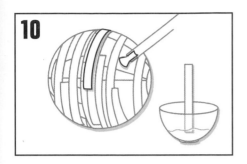

10

Papier mâché one layer of newspaper over the areas that have been taped – the join and the pole insertion. This will make it extra secure.

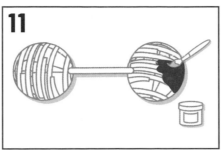

11

Once the papier mâché is dry, paint the weights black.

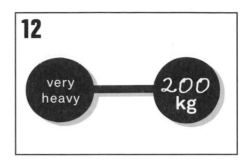

12

Finally, paint on the details using white paint: '200 kg', 'very heavy', 'strong people only'.

Amazing feats of superhuman strength!

Toy lion

YOU WILL NEED

- Prepared templates (page 139)
- 50 x 30 cm (19¾ x 12 in) piece of plain yellow cotton
- 50 x 30 cm (19¾ x 12 in) piece of striped cotton
- 3 strips of yellow felt – approx 2 cm (1 in) wide and 30 cm (12 in) long or a length of yellow ribbon
- Wadding or cotton wool
- Needle and thread
- Dressmaker's carbon paper
- Black fabric paint or a black fabric marker
- Rice
- Scissors

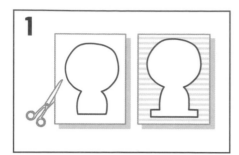

1

Place the front body template on plain yellow cotton and the back template on a stripy cotton and trace around it with tailor's chalk or a fabric pencil. Cut out the shapes leaving a 1 cm (½ in) gap from the traced line to allow for the hems.

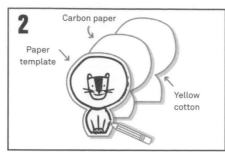

2

Take the lion face template and cut out just outside the outer line. Lay this paper template on your fabric, right-side facing up, with carbon paper sandwiched between the two and lightly trace the lion. Repeat this step for the lion's back details.

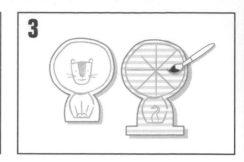

3

With black fabric paint or fabric marker, paint on the lion's features, following your traced lines. Follow the instructions on your fabric paint/marker. Allow to dry.

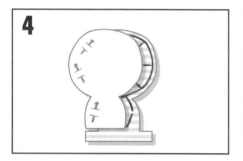

4

Align the two pieces of fabric at the top, with the painted sides facing inwards, and pin together.

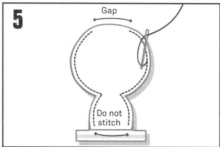

5

Sew the two sides together, leaving a 5 cm (2 in) gap at the top, and do not stitch the bottom.

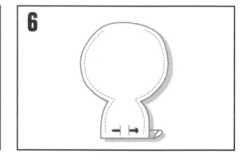

6

Pinch and align the two straight bottom edges, pin and sew together. The back stripy fabric will now be puckered – this is ok.

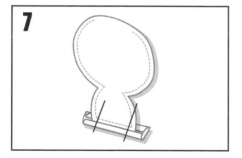

7

Flatten out the puckered bottom so that it is horizontal and the main 'body' section is vertical. Sew across the bottom section on the purple lines shown, with a tight running stitch. Note: the stitches should be just inside the 'body corner' stitching.

8

Snip the excess fabric and then turn right-side out, through the gap at the top.

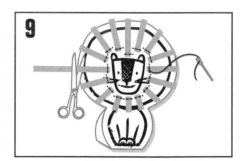

9

Take a strip of felt and, starting close to the face, sew it on to the head to create the mane. Cut the strip off at the edge of the head, then repeat. Where the strips overlap the whiskers, just mark the whiskers with fabric marker on the felt.

10

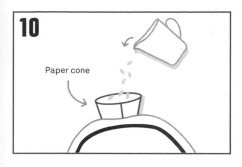

Paper cone

Fill the lower part of the body with rice through the gap in the lion's head. Fill up to the top of the leg line, to make a base for the lion to stand on.

11

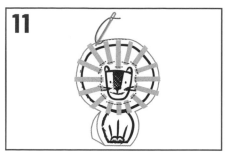

Stuff the top half of the lion tightly with wadding or cotton wool. Finally, stitch the gap at the top of the head closed with a small hidden stitch.

Animal masks:
bear and fox

Tepee

Tail

Toy fox

Animal paws

Woodland animals

Leaf bunting

Animal wall faces

Fox ears

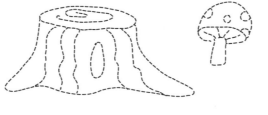

Tepee

YOU WILL NEED

- 4 m (13 ft) of fabric
- Hula hoop (the largest you can find)
- Natural rope (such as washing line rope)
- 12 toggles or buttons
- Needle and thread
- Scissors
- Pins
- Tailor's chalk or fabric pencil
- Long ruler
- Hemming tape
- Iron

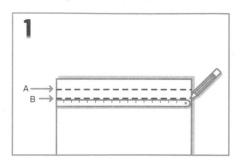

Lay the fabric out working side down, making sure the cut ends are straight and neat. Using tailor's chalk or fabric pencil, mark the width of your ruler from one short end of the fabric (A), then mark a ruler's width from the first line (B).

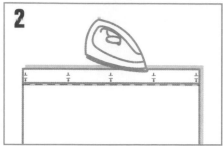

Fold along the first marked line (A), pin and iron. Remove the pins.

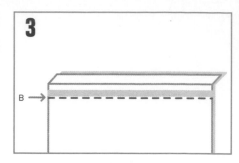

Position the hemming tape a few millimetres (¼ in) above the second marked line (B). Fold back down, pin the ends and follow the instructions on the hemming tape package to secure the hem.

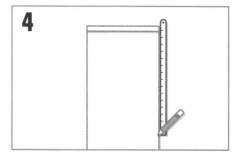

Working side down, carefully measure and mark 96.5 cm (38 in) from the newly hemmed end.

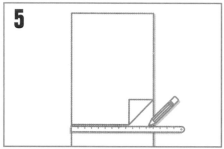

Fold at the mark, align the edges carefully and mark a line where the fabric fold ends. This is line A.

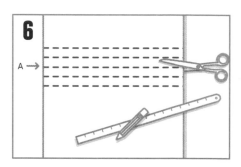

Mark two ruler widths on both sides of line A. Cut along line A. You now have two pieces of fabric.

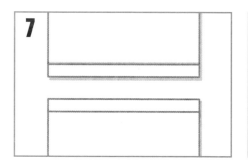

Repeat steps 3 and 4 to hem the ends of the first and second pieces of fabric.

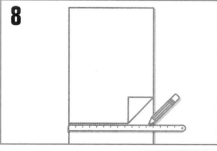

Repeat steps 5 and 6 to determine the length of the second piece of fabric, and cut to the correct length. Repeat steps 2–4 for the final hem. You now have two pieces of hemmed fabric.

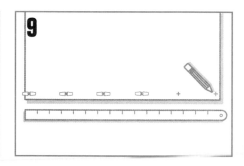

Take one piece of fabric and, starting at one side of the first hem, working side up, mark halfway up the hem 2.5 cm (1 in) and draw a line in tailor's chalk. Then make four marks 22 cm (8⅔ in) apart along that line, and finally mark 2.5 cm (1 in) from the last mark. Repeat for the other piece of fabric. Sew on a button or toggle at each mark.

10

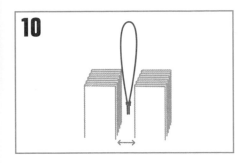

Take the other end of both pieces of fabric and fold neatly, as shown. Place a book on top to stop them from unfolding. Tie the rope as shown and position between the two folded pieces of fabric.

11

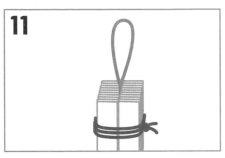

Wrap a rope very tightly around the two pieces of folded fabric and the first rope, and knot securely. The length of the rope used will depend on where you wish to hang the tepee.

12

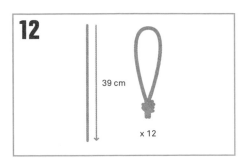

39 cm

x 12

Make 12 fastening loops from 39 cm (15½in) lengths of rope, as shown using a reef knot.

13

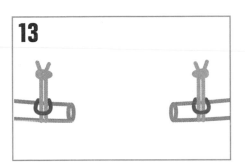

Pull the hula hoop apart at its join. Attach the fastening loops at even intervals around the hoop.

14

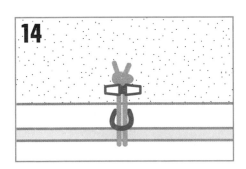

Fix the tepee top to the base with the toggles and loops.

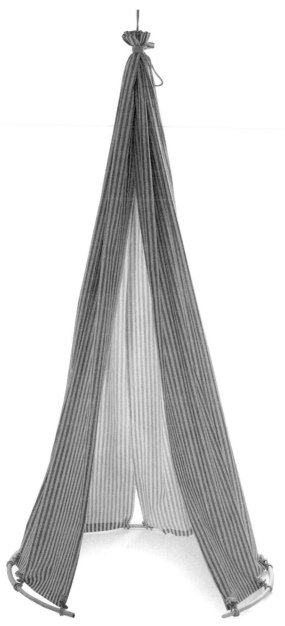

Animal masks: bear and fox

YOU WILL NEED

- Prepared templates (page 142) scaled according to the size of your child's face
- Felt in various colours: white, black, orange, red, brown, blue and pale pink
- Pieces of elastic long enough to reach around your child's head (one piece for each mask)
- Needle and thread
- Scissors or craft knife
- Fabric glue
- Black fabric marker (for the fox)

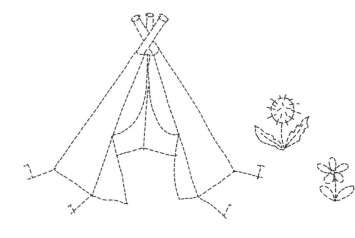

Bear →

1

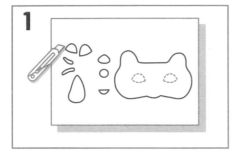

Prepare and cut out the template.

2

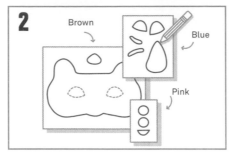

Brown

Blue

Pink

Draw around the templates on to felt of the appropriate colour.

3

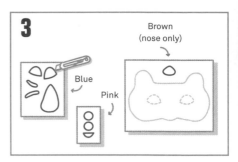

Brown (nose only)

Blue

Pink

Cut out the pink, blue and brown (nose only) shapes from the felt.

4

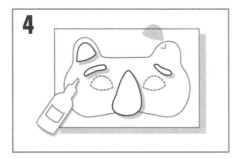

Apply a layer of fabric glue to the reverse side of the blue felt and stick it to the brown felt in the correct positions.

5

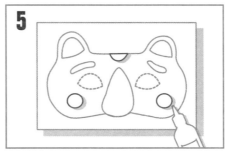

Stick the pink felt shapes to the brown felt.

6

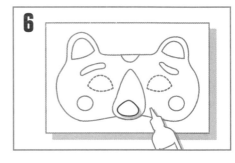

Stick the brown nose to the blue snout.

7

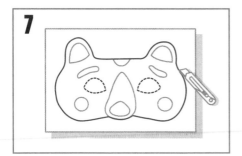

Cut out the brown face shape, including the eye holes.

8

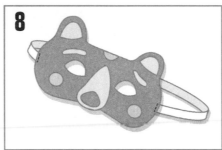

Finally, attach the elastic to the sides of the mask with a few very secure stitches.

Fox →

1

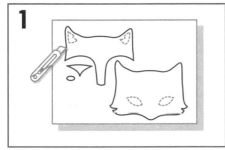

Prepare and cut out the template.

2

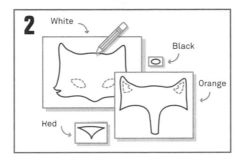

White
Black
Orange
Red

Draw around the templates on to felt of the appropriate colour.

3

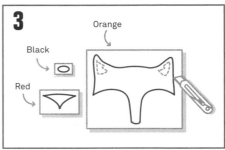

Orange
Black
Red

Cut out the orange, red and black shapes from the felt – including the ear cut outs on the orange felt.

4

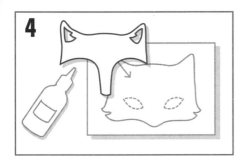

Apply a layer of fabric glue to the reverse side of the orange felt and stick it to the white felt, aligning the ears and the top of the head.

5

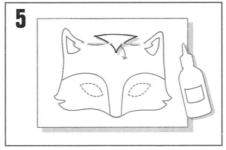

Stick the red piece of felt to the orange, making sure the top edges meet.

6

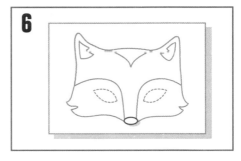

Stick the black nose to the orange felt at the bottom of the face.

7

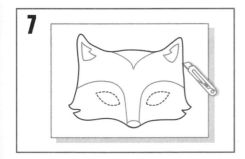

Cut out the white shape, including the eye holes.

8

Mark the details with a black fabric marker – eyes, whiskers, etc. Be creative!

9

Finally, attach the elastic to the sides of the mask with a few very secure stitches.

Tail

YOU WILL NEED

- Prepared template (page 141)
- Furry fabric 26 cm (10 ¼ in) wide and 31 cm (12 ½ in) long
- 1.5 m (5 ft) length of 15 mm (½ in) ribbon
- Wadding or cotton wool
- Needle and thread
- Pins
- Tailor's chalk or fabric pencil
- Craft knife and cutting board
- Fabric glue

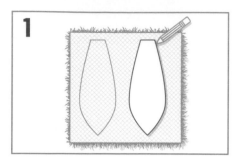

Draw around the template twice on to the fur fabric fur side down.

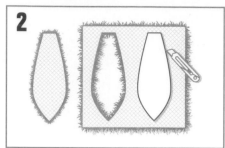

Using a craft knife, cut the pieces out using short, shallow cuts and avoiding the fur pile.

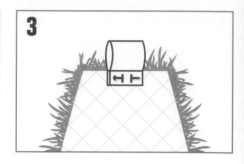

To make the tail loop, position and pin 10 cm (4 in) of ribbon, as shown.

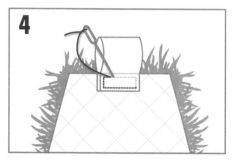

Using running stitch, sew the ribbon in place. Try to avoid catching the fur with your needle.

Squeeze fabric glue on to the back of the tail pieces, as shown, being careful not to get it on the fur.

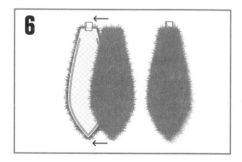

Press the two pieces together and place between heavy books to dry.

Lightly stuff the tail with wadding or cotton wool.

Squeeze fabric glue around the gap at the top.

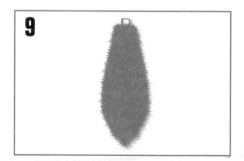

Press together and place between heavy books to dry.

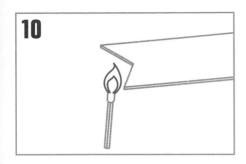

10

Melt the ends of the remaining ribbon with a match or your stove, to stop them from fraying.

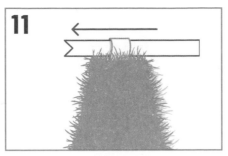

11

Thread the ribbon through the tail loop and tie it around your little animal's waist.

Be bright-eyed and bushy-tailed!

Animal wall faces

YOU WILL NEED

- Cardboard box
- Newspaper and papier mâché paste mix (page 11)
- Scissors
- Pencil
- Masking tape
- White, black/brown, grey, blue and pink paint and paintbrushes
- Black/brown marker (optional)

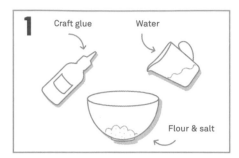

1 Craft glue Water Flour & salt

In a bowl or other container make up a batch of papier mâché paste mix (see page 11) and set aside.

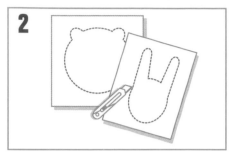

2

Draw simple animal faces and ears on to a cardboard box, and cut them out. We chose a bear and a rabbit.

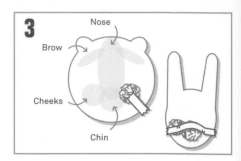

3 Nose Brow Cheeks Chin

Start building up the shape of the face by scrunching up newspaper and taping it down with masking tape. Think about the brows, nose, chin, cheeks, snout and so on. It doesn't have to be perfect!

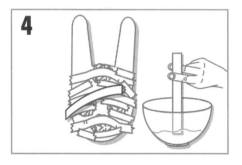

4

Once you're happy with the shape of the face, dip long strips of newspaper into the paste mix and start sticking them on to the face. After dipping each strip of newspaper, slide it between two fingers to rid the paper of any excess mix. Cover the whole face with one layer of newspaper, allow to dry, then add another layer. You can also dip squares of newspaper in the mix and scrunch into balls to help build up the nose.

TIP

After applying the first layer of papier mâché, roll one of the rabbit ears forwards a little and allow to dry leaning against a cup.

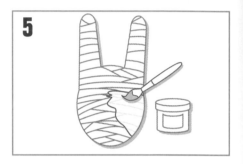

5

Once the papier mâché is completely dry, paint the heads white, allow to dry, then add another coat of white paint.

6

When the white paint is completely dry, you can add the animal's face and features using paint and a fine paintbrush, or a marker. Then mount the animal heads on the wall.

If you go down to the
woods today...

Animal paws

YOU WILL NEED

- Wristwarmers, mittens or fingerless gloves
- Furry fabric approximately 20 x 20 cm (8 x 8 in)
- Paper
- Pencil
- Scissors
- Tailor's chalk or fabric pencil
- Craft knife and cutting board
- Fabric glue

1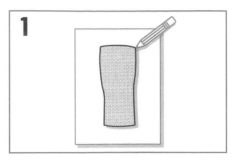

Draw around one of your gloves with a pencil on to a piece of paper.

2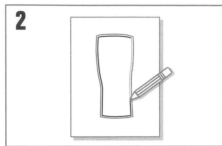

Draw a line around the template 0.5 cm (¼in) inside the original line.

3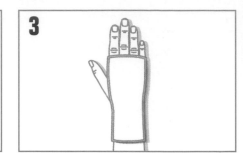

Cut out the smaller outline and check against your glove for size. Put the glove on to double-check.

4

Draw around the template on to the fur fabric, fur side down. Turn the template over and draw around it once more.

5

With a craft knife, cut the pieces out using short, shallow cuts and avoiding the fur pile.

6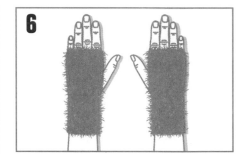

Put the glove on to work out which piece is for which hand.

7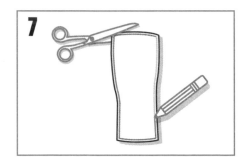

Cut off about 0.5 cm (¼ in) all the way around your original paper template.

8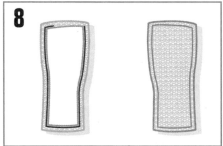

Draw around the new template with tailor's chalk or fabric pencil.

9

Squeeze fabric glue along the chalk line and on to the edges of the fur.

10

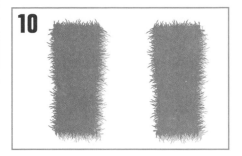

Press the pieces together and leave between heavy books overnight to dry.

Toy fox

YOU WILL NEED

- Prepared templates (page 143)
- Old wool (or wool-mix) jumper
- Wadding or cotton wool
- Sewing needle and matching thread
- Scissors
- Pins
- Freezer paper
- Marker pen
- Black fabric paint
- Iron
- Washing machine

1

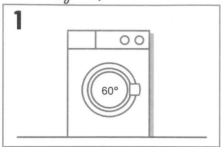

Put the jumper into the washing machine and run a 60°C (140°F) cycle. This will felt the fabric. Allow to dry.

2

Prepare and cut out the templates.

3

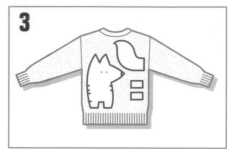

Position the templates on one side of the jumper to make sure they all fit.

4

On a discreet part of the jumper, check that the marker pen won't seep through the fabric. Then draw around each template.

5

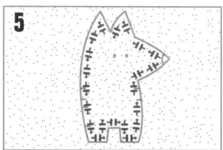

Following your lines, pin the body shape through both sides of the jumper.

6

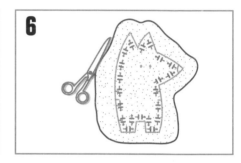

Roughly cut it out, leaving at least 1 cm (½ in) around the lines.

7

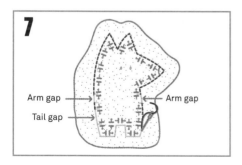

Arm gap

Arm gap

Tail gap

Backstitch around the lines, making sure to leave the marked gaps unstitched.

8

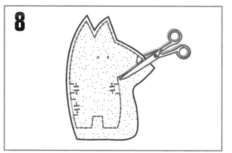

Trim the seams neatly to leave 0.5 cm (¼ in) around the stitched line.

9

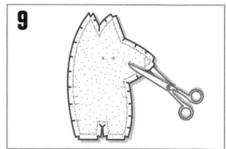

Snip the curved edges and corners.

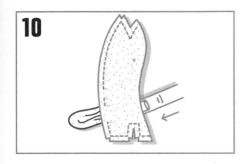

10

Turn the body the right way out through the tail gap.

11

Push out the corners using the wrong end of a pencil.

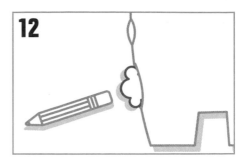

12

Stuff with wadding or cotton wool, keeping it soft (don't over-stuff!)

Tail ⟶

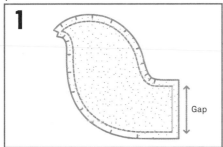

1

Gap

For the tail, repeat steps 5–10 using the tail templates. Leave the marked gap unstitched.

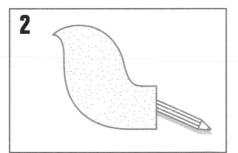

2

Push out the corners.

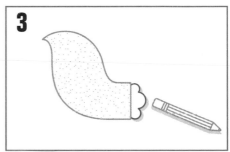

3

Stuff with wadding or cotton wool, keeping it soft.

arms ⟶

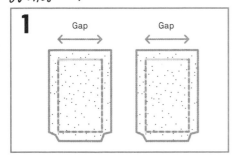

1

Gap   Gap

For the arms, repeat steps 5–10 using the arms template. Make sure you make two arms. Leave the marked gap unstitched.

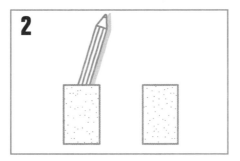

2

Push out the corners.

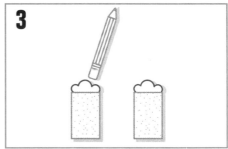

3

Stuff with wadding or cotton wool, keeping it soft.

1

To join the parts, position them and pin on to the body. Start with the tail.

2

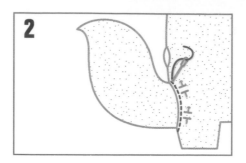

Sew into place using close running stitch.

3

Position and pin the arms into place.

4

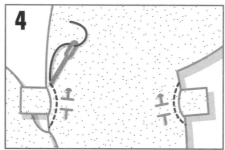

Sew the arms to the body using close running stitch.

Paint →

1

Carefully trim any excess fluff from the surface of the fabric where you want to put the eyes, nose, mouth and tail markings. Do this by holding the scissors flat against the fabric as you snip.

2

Dip the end of your pen into fabric paint a few millimeters. Then carefully press into place. Allow to dry.

3

Carefully trim any excess fluff from the surface of the fabric where you want to put the nose and then paint it on.

Hello Mr Fox!

Fox ears

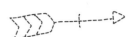

YOU WILL NEED

- Prepared templates (page 143)
- Woolly hat or beanie
- Furry fabric 30 x 30 cm (12 x 12 in)
- Needle and thread
- Scissors
- Pins
- Tailor's chalk or fabric pencil
- Craft knife and cutting board
- Fabric glue (if using Technique b)

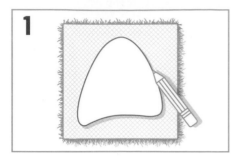

1 Orientate the fur so the nap is pointing upwards. Fur side down, draw around the ear template using tailor's chalk or pencil. Repeat for the other ear.

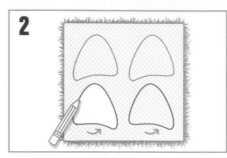

2 Turn the template over and draw around it twice more.

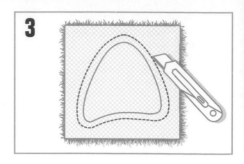

3 Keeping the fabric fur side down, place it on a cutting surface. Leaving roughly 1.5 cm ($^5/_8$ in) around the drawn line, cut out the ears using a very sharp craft knife. Use small strokes, and try to cut the woven backing only, avoiding the fur. Rub the edges gently to remove any excess fur; you may want to do this over a bin or outside.

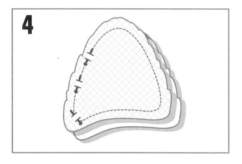

4 Take one of each of the sides of the ears and pin together all the way around, with the fur on the inside.

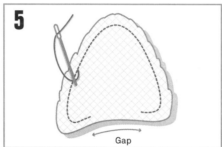

5 Backstitch the two pieces together, leaving the gap indicated on the template. Unpin and turn the right way out. Gently brush the seams to encourage the fur to come out.

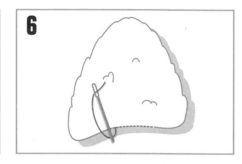

6 Using hidden stitch, stitch closed the remaining gap. Repeat steps 3–6 for the other ear.

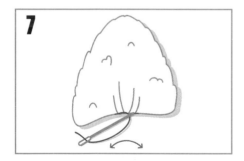

7 Pinch together a small part of the ear in the middle at the bottom and put a stitch through both sides to draw them towards each other. This will give the ear a slightly curved shape. Repeat for the other ear.

8 Place the hat over a large jar or something similar that will hold it upright.

9 Position and pin the ears on the hat. At this point, try the hat on your little woodland animal's head to check the position. Be careful of sharp pins!

TIP

You may find that the ears need to be placed further forward than you think.

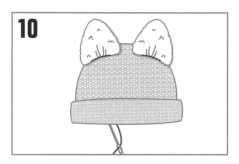

10

Starting on the inside of the hat, stitch the ears on tightly using running stitch. Fasten off inside the hat and repeat for the other ear. Time to play woodland animals!

Technique b →

3b

When cutting out the template, use all the same techniques as described in step 3 but, instead of cutting outside of the drawn line, cut on the drawn line.

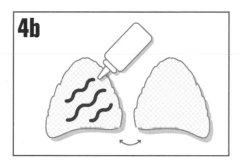

4b

Instead of sewing the ears together, take one of each of the sides of the ears and glue together using fabric glue or adhesive. Be careful not to get glue on the fur, but go as close to the edge as you can. Repeat for the other ear. Place the ears under a pile of heavy books overnight to dry. Then attach the ears to the hat as described in steps 8–10.

TIP

Use technique B if you are using high-quality, longer fur.

Prick up your ears!

Leaf bunting

YOU WILL NEED

- 60 x 60 cm (2 x 2 ft) piece of plain cotton fabric
- Approx. 2 m (6 ft) string, or more if you want longer bunting
- Needle and matching thread
- Scissors
- Cling film
- Craft glue
- Acrylic paint, either in various shades of green or in reds and oranges
- Paintbrushes

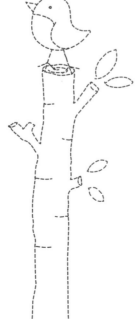

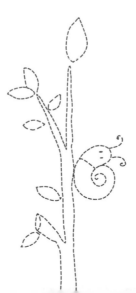

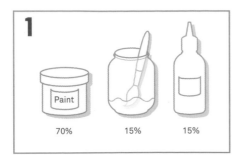

1 In a clean container, mix the paint with a little water and craft glue – approximately 70 per cent paint and 15 per cent each of water and glue.

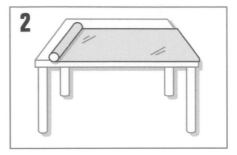

2 Cover a flat surface bigger than the fabric (such as a table or worktop) with cling film, and wrap the cling film over the edges to protect it.

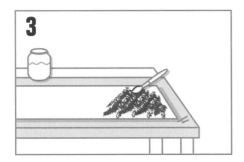

3 Lay the fabric flat on the prepared surface and paint the fabric with your paint mix.

TIP

Slowly add different paint colours into your mix to create a variation in colour.

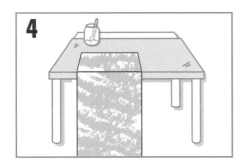

4 Once the fabric is completely painted, hang it over the edges of the table and allow to dry.

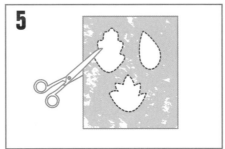

5 When the cotton is dry, cut out leaf shapes approximately 12 x 9 cm (4¾ x 3½ in).

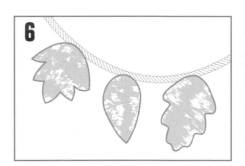

6 Sew the leaves on to the string, leaving an 8–10 cm (3–4 in) gap between them.

Pirate moustache and beard

ENLARGE 175%

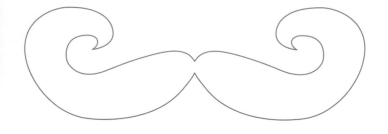

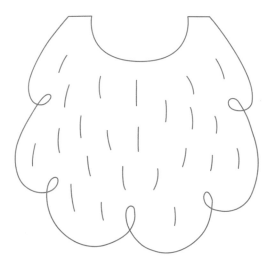

Pirate hat

TEMPLATE 100%

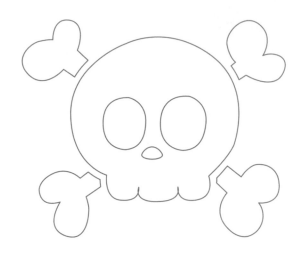

Pirate hook

ENLARGE 250%

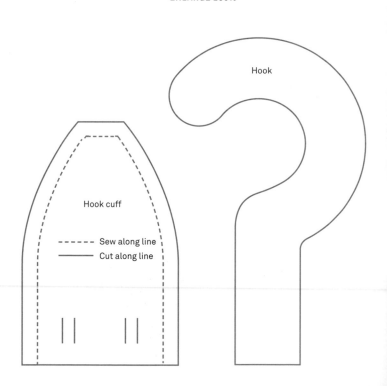

Hook

Hook cuff

- - - - Sew along line

——— Cut along line

Pirate eyepatch

TEMPLATE 100%

Sail
ENLARGE 500%

Pirate treasure bag label
TEMPLATE 100%

Telescope
ENLARGE 300%

Eye piece

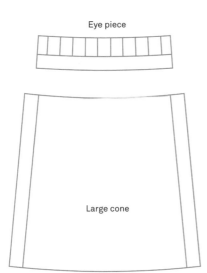

Large cone

Small cone

Large cone end 2

Large cone end 1

Mini pirate

ENLARGE 200%

Head

Body

Arm 1

Arm 2

MUM

Moustache

Eyepatch

Beard

Pirate hat

Wave bedhead

ENLARGE 400%

Line up when
printing edge
of A4 page →

Line up when
printing edge
of A4 page →

Circus letters

INCREASE TO FIT YOUR WOOD PANEL

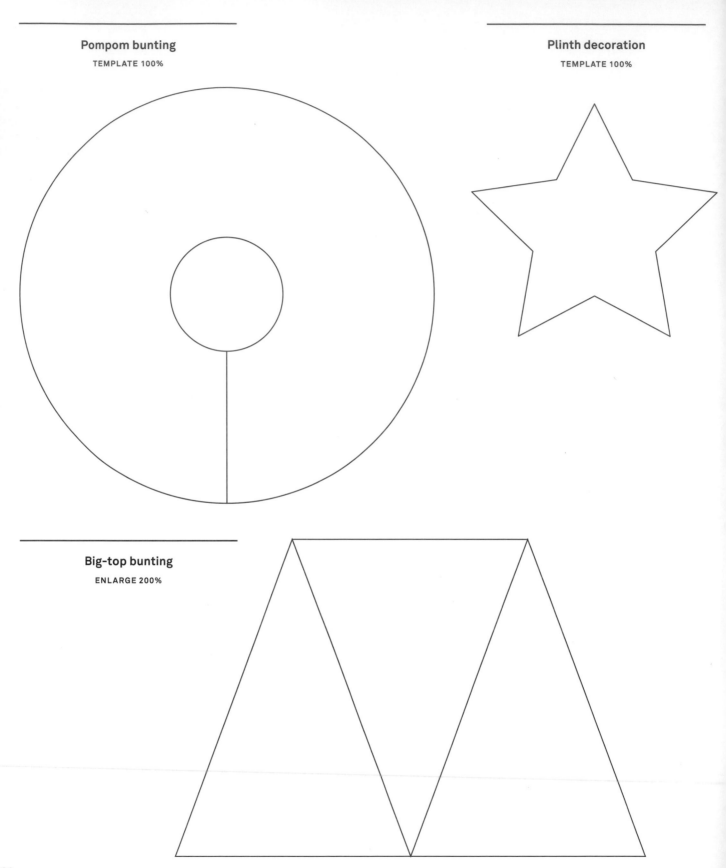

Pompom bunting
TEMPLATE 100%

Plinth decoration
TEMPLATE 100%

Big-top bunting
ENLARGE 200%

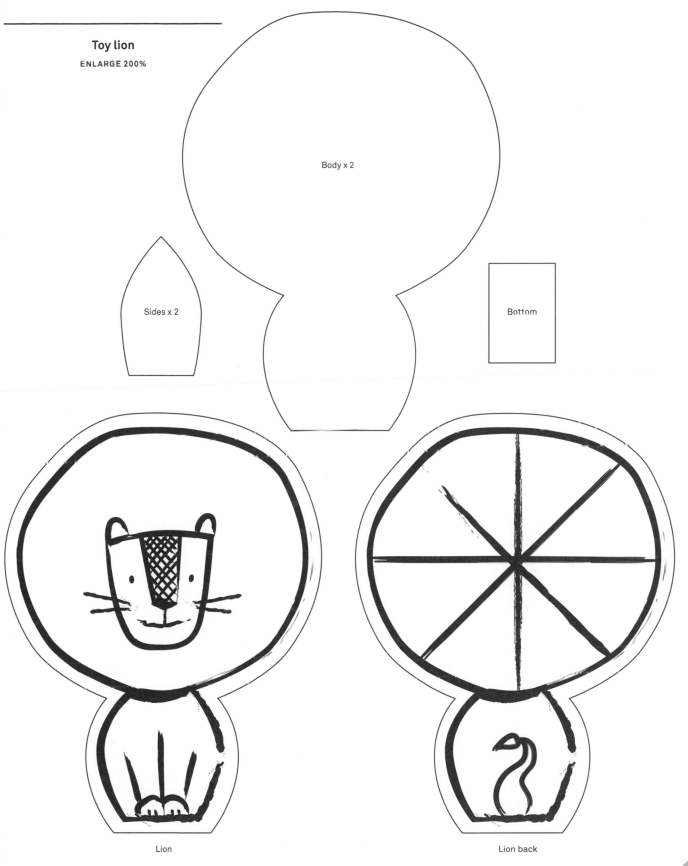

Toy lion

ENLARGE 200%

Body x 2

Sides x 2

Bottom

Lion

Lion back

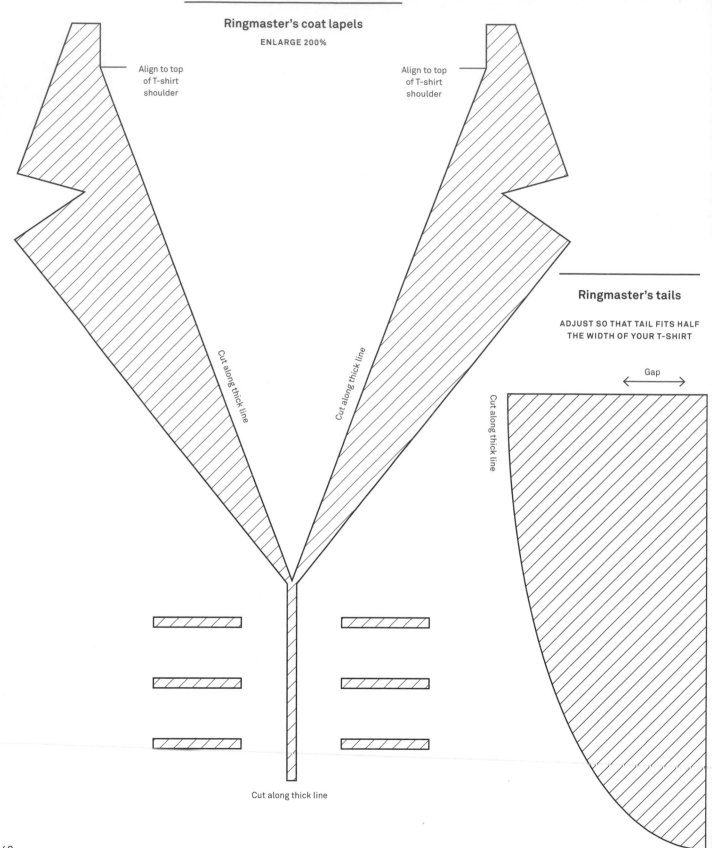

Ringmaster's coat lapels
ENLARGE 200%

Align to top
of T-shirt
shoulder

Align to top
of T-shirt
shoulder

Cut along thick line

Cut along thick line

Ringmaster's tails

**ADJUST SO THAT TAIL FITS HALF
THE WIDTH OF YOUR T-SHIRT**

Gap

Cut along thick line

Cut along thick line

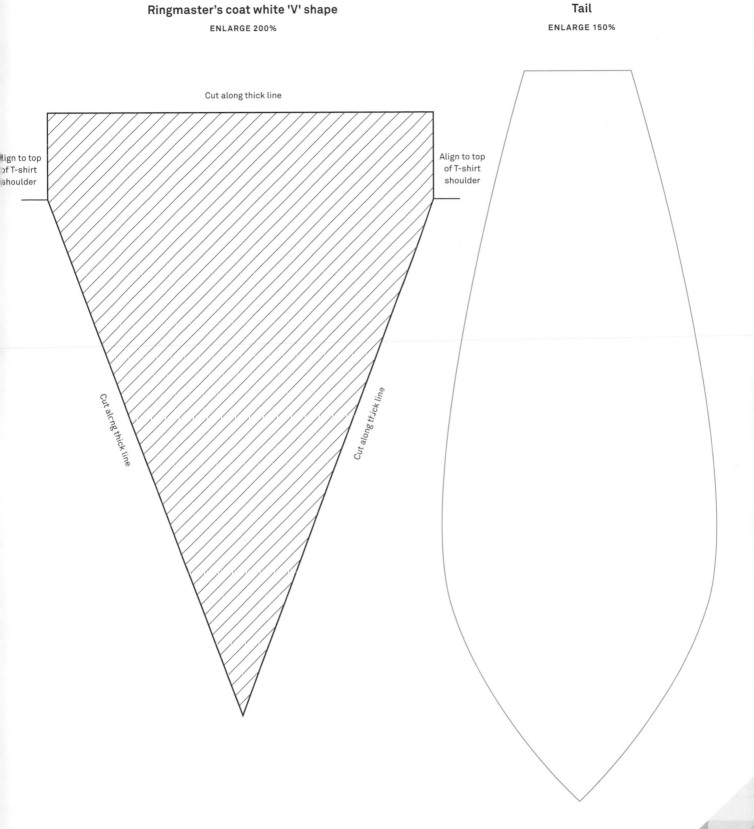

Ringmaster's coat white 'V' shape
ENLARGE 200%

Tail
ENLARGE 150%

Cut along thick line

Align to top of T-shirt shoulder

Align to top of T-shirt shoulder

Cut along thick line

Cut along thick line

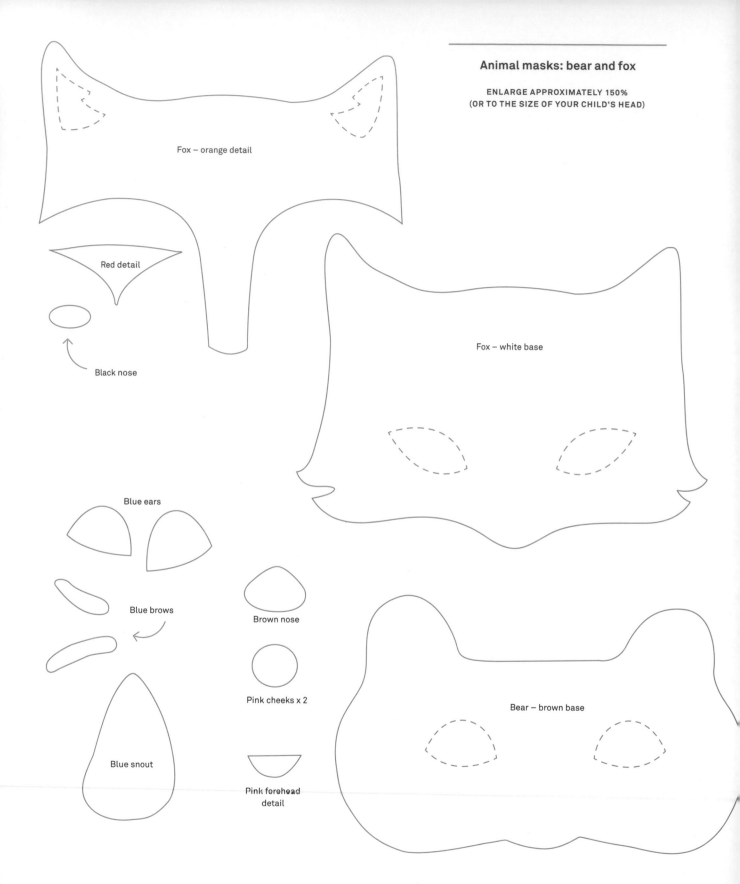

Fox – orange detail

Red detail

Black nose

Blue ears

Blue brows

Brown nose

Blue snout

Pink cheeks x 2

Pink forehead detail

Fox – white base

Bear – brown base

Animal masks: bear and fox

ENLARGE APPROXIMATELY 150%
(OR TO THE SIZE OF YOUR CHILD'S HEAD)

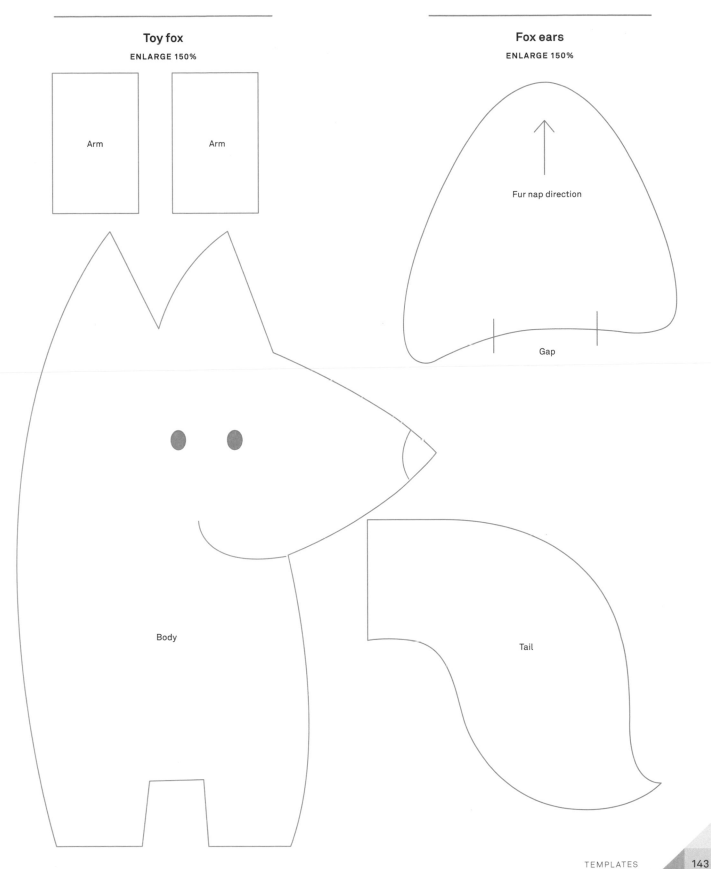

Toy fox
ENLARGE 150%

Arm

Arm

Body

Fox ears
ENLARGE 150%

Fur nap direction

Gap

Tail

Acknowledgements

I would like to thank Jill Bee, my mum, who was my inspiration for the book. She has taught me all I know and she gave me an amazing childhood filled with creativity and skills that have shaped my life. Jemma and I would never have completed the book without your unquestioning help and support so thank you, Jilly!

Also, I want to thank Jemma for the most productive chat ever on the balcony at flat 4!

Stella

Firstly, I would like to thank Stella, my lovely co-author. Without her, this book wouldn't have been possible, let alone thought of! Thank you, Stel, for your creativity, drive and encouragement.

I would also like to give thanks to my supportive partner, Paul – for allowing our house to become an activity testing-site! – and to my kind and loving mum – if I hadn't come home from school to new costumes and fairy wings, my creative childhood may not have become a working reality.

Finally, I second Stella's thanks to her very clever mum, Jilly. Your help was incredible and much appreciated.

Jemma